DAYS TO CELEBRATE

A Full Year of Poetry, People, Holidays,
History, Fascinating Facts, and More

WRITTEN AND EDITED BY
LEE BENNETT HOPKINS

ILLUSTRATED BY
STEPHEN ALCORN

Greenwillow Books, *An Imprint of HarperCollins*Publishers

To Donna Lea and Anthony G. Venturi—
for a lifetime of celebrations

—L. B. H.

For my mother, con eterna gratitudine

—S. A.

Days to Celebrate: A Full Year of Poetry, People, Holidays, History, Fascinating Facts, and More
Copyright © 2005 by Lee Bennett Hopkins. Illustrations copyright © 2005 by Stephen Alcorn. The individual poets represented in this volume hold the copyright to their poems. Page 110 constitutes an extension of the copyright page. All rights reserved. No part of this book may be used or reproduced in any manner whatsoever without written permission except in the case of brief quotations embodied in critical articles and reviews. Manufactured in China. For information address HarperCollins Children's Books, a division of HarperCollins Publishers, 1350 Avenue of the Americas, New York, NY 10019. www.harperchildrens.com

Library of Congress Cataloging-in-Publication Data

Hopkins, Lee Bennett. Days to celebrate: a full year of poetry, people, holidays, history, fascinating facts, and more / Lee Bennett Hopkins. p. cm. "Greenwillow Books." Summary: Provides a listing of events, births of famous people, and holidays, with information and poetry about the twelve months of the year. ISBN 0-06-000765-6 (trade). ISBN 0-06-000766-4 (lib. bdg.). 1. Almanacs, Children's. [1. Almanacs.] I. Title: A full year of poetry, people, holidays, history, fascinating facts, and more. II. Title. AY81.J8H67 2004 051—dc22 2003049288

First Edition 10 9 8 7 6 5 4 3 2 1　　Greenwillow Books

Contents

Introduction

Days to Celebrate takes you on a journey through the twelve months of the year—a trip bursting with people, holidays, historical events, poetry, and more.

As you travel through each month, you will find birth dates of famous people who have contributed to society in so many rich and welcome ways—artists, musicians, dancers, entertainers, poets, writers, scientists, politicians, religious leaders, and sports figures. (A few birth dates are followed by question marks because dates were never recorded, birth certificates were lost, or people were unwilling to reveal their true ages.) You will meet men and women who accomplished daring human feats, blazed new paths, advanced human culture, and invented incredible everyday things from windshield wipers to toothpaste tubes to computers.

Page by page you will encounter a wide array of holidays and celebrations, from a bean-throwing festival in Japan to America's National Poetry Month. And you will discover a host of "firsts"—when and where the first McDonald's, the first Laundromat, and the first movie theater opened, for example—as well as world records, such as the banana split that measured 4.55 miles long and the game of Twister that was played by 4,160 people.

To round out the year there is information on each month—how it was named, what its flower and birthstone are, which zodiac sign is associated with it; a surprising weather statistic; and a quotation from a renowned individual born during the month.

And there is poetry, too: a treasure trove of work created by past masters and contemporary poets writing about people, holidays, seasons, and fascinating subjects—fossils, pencils, subways, baseball, radishes, earmuffs, and windy nights.

Stephen Alcorn's spirited artwork adorns each page with imaginative, interpretive, bold compositions.

I hope these entries and poems spark your interest and take you on a voyage of further exploration.

Right now, if you are as curious as I am (and if you haven't already done so), I am sure you will look at your birth date to see what has happened on that day over the years. It is a good place to start and to give you more reasons to make every day a special one.

Happy reading!

—*Lee Bennett Hopkins*

Scarborough, New York

January

Martin Luther King, Jr. Day: 3rd Monday

Chinese New Year: Between January 21 and February 19, based on the lunar calendar.

1 *New Year's Day*
1735 Birth date: Paul Revere, American patriot

2
1788 Georgia: 4th state to enter the Union

3
1888 Drinking straw patented by Marvin Stone

1892 Birth date: John Ronald Reul ("J. R. R.") Tolkien, English author of *The Hobbit* and *The Lord of the Rings*

1938 Birth date: Alma Flor Ada, Cuban author

1959 Alaska: 49th state to enter the Union

4
1785 Birth date: Jacob Ludwig Carl Grimm, German collector of fairy tales

1809 Birth date: Louis Braille, inventor of the Braille system for the blind

1896 Utah: 45th state to enter the Union

9
1788 Connecticut: 5th state to enter the Union

1913 Birth date: Richard Milhous Nixon, 37th U.S. president

10
1901 Oil discovered in Beaumont, TX, begins the great oil boom

11
1755 Birth date: Alexander Hamilton, patriot, first secretary of the U.S. treasury

1815 Birth date: Sir John Alexander Macdonald, first prime minister of Canada

1839 Birth date: Eugenio María de Hostos, Puerto Rican patriot, author

12
1737 Birth date: John Hancock, first signer of the Declaration of Independence

1932 Hattie W. Caraway from Arkansas becomes the first U.S. woman senator

17
1706 Birth date: Benjamin Franklin, patriot, inventor, author

18
1882 Birth date: Alan Alexander ("A. A.") Milne, English author of *Winnie-the-Pooh*

19
1807 Birth date: Robert E. Lee, Confederate general

1809 Birth date: Edgar Allan Poe, author, poet

1825 Tin can for storing food patented by Ezra Daggett and Thomas Kensett

1839 Birth date: Paul Cézanne, French artist

20
1892: Basketball first played, Springfield, MA

25
1961 John F. Kennedy, Jr., holds first live televised news conference by a U.S. president

26
1837 Michigan: 26th state to enter the Union

1892 Birth date: Bessie Coleman, aviator

27
1756 Birth date: Wolfgang Amadeus Mozart, Austrian composer

1832 Birth date: Charles Lutwidge Dodgson ("Lewis Carroll"), English author

28
1878 First commercial telephone switchboard installed; serves 21 customers in New Haven, CT

Benjamin Franklin said:

"Never leave that till tomorrow which you can do today."

—From *Poor Richard's Almanack*

From the Latin Januarius. *Ancient Romans named the first month of the year after Janus, a Roman god. Pictured with two faces, Janus could look back into the past and forward into the future.*

FLOWER: CARNATION
BIRTHSTONE: GARNET
ZODIAC SIGN: AQUARIUS, THE WATER BEARER (JANUARY 20–FEBRUARY 18)
AQUARIANS ENJOY FREEDOM, INDEPENDENCE, BREAKING NEW GROUND WITH UNIQUE THOUGHTS AND IDEAS.

---

5 *George Washington Carver Day*

1925 Nellie Tayloe Ross of Wyoming becomes the first U.S. woman governor

1931 Birth date: Alvin Ailey, Jr., dancer, choreographer

6

1412 Birth date: Joan of Arc, French patriot and saint

1878 Birth date: Carl Sandburg, poet, author

1912 New Mexico: 47th state to enter the Union

7

1800 Birth date: Millard Fillmore, 13th U.S. president

8

1935 Birth date: Elvis Aaron Presley, singer, actor

13

1926 Birth date: Michael Bond, creator of *Paddington Bear* books

14

1886 Birth date: Hugh Lofting, author of *Doctor Dolittle* books

15

1929 Birth date: Martin Luther King, Jr., civil rights leader

1967 First Super Bowl football game played, Los Angeles, CA

16

1908? Birth date: Ethel (Agnes Zimmerman) Merman, one of the leading Broadway musical performers of the twentieth century

---

21

1941 Birth date: Plácido Domingo, opera singer

22

1961 Wilma Rudolph, Olympic gold medalist and track star, sets world indoor record in women's 60-yard dash

23

1849 Elizabeth Blackwell becomes the first woman doctor in the U.S.

24

1925 Birth date: Maria Tallchief, ballet dancer

29

1843 Birth date: William McKinley, 25th U.S. president

1861 Kansas: 34th state to enter the Union

30

1882 Birth date: Franklin Delano Roosevelt, 32nd U.S. president

31

1797 Birth date: Franz Peter Schubert, Austrian composer

1919 Birth date: Jack ("Jackie") Roosevelt Robinson, baseball player

---

WEATHER REPORT

On January 23, 1971, in Prospect Creek Camp, Alaska, the mercury dropped to minus 80 degrees, setting the record for the coldest day ever in the United States.

From
In Memoriam

Alfred, Lord Tennyson

Ring out, wild bells, to the wild sky,
  The flying cloud, the frosty light:
  The year is dying in the night;
Ring out, wild bells, and let them die.

Ring out the old, ring in the new,
  Ring, happy bells, across the snow:
  The year is going, let him go;
Ring out the false, ring in the true.

9

January 6: Birth date: Carl Sandburg (1878–1967)

Sandburg wrote more than eight hundred verses during his lifetime. He also wrote wonderful definitions of poetry. One is: "Poetry is the journal of a sea animal living on land, wanting to fly in the air."

His work celebrates the day-to-day lives of ordinary people and common objects—bubbles, balloons, tractors, toes, fish, fog—even . . .

Arithmetic *Carl Sandburg*

Arithmetic is where numbers fly like pigeons in and out of your head.

Arithmetic tells you how many you lose or win if you know how many you
    had before you lost or won.

Arithmetic is seven eleven all good children go to heaven—or five six
    bundle of sticks.

Arithmetic is numbers you squeeze from your head to your hand to your
    pencil to your paper till you get the answer.

Arithmetic is where the answer is right and everything is nice and you can
    look out of the window and see the blue sky—or the answer is wrong
    and you have to start all over and try again and see how it comes out
    this time.

If you take a number and double it and double it again and then double
    it a few more times, the number gets bigger and bigger and goes
    higher and higher and only arithmetic can tell you what the number
    is when you decide to quit doubling.

Arithmetic is where you have to multiply—and you carry the multiplication
    table in your head and hope you won't lose it.

If you have two animal crackers, one good and one bad, and you eat one
    and a striped zebra with streaks all over him eats the other, how many
    animal crackers will you have if somebody offers you five six seven
    and you say No no no and you say Nay nay nay and you say Nix
    nix nix?

If you ask your mother for one fried egg for breakfast and she gives you
    two fried eggs and you eat both of them, who is better in arithmetic,
    you or your mother?

January 15: Birth date: Martin Luther King, Jr. (1929–1968)

One of America's greatest visionaries, King was at the forefront of the civil rights movement from the mid-1950s until his assassination on April 4, 1968, in Memphis, Tennessee. He was instrumental in bringing about the Civil Rights Act of 1964, which protects the rights of African-Americans to live, work, and vote without discrimination. He received the Nobel Prize for Peace in 1964.

In 1983, the U.S. Congress designated the third Monday in January a federal holiday to honor his ideals and lifelong work in civil rights.

"Say that I was a drum major for justice."
—*Martin Luther King, Jr.*

A Question for Martin

Nikki Grimes

Why, Martin?
Why did you spend yourself
till all the gold
was gone?
Why march in Montgomery,
Selma, and Washington, D.C.,
till your drum-major's uniform
frayed at the cuffs?
History proved
we didn't love you enough.
So why, when God tapped you
on the shoulder,
and gave you that drum
to beat for justice,
why did you heed the call
at all?
Did you wake in the night,
ears bursting and bloody
from the rising crescendo
of your people's cry?
Is that what made you
willing to die?

January 17: Birth date: Benjamin Franklin (1706–1790)

Franklin, a self-educated man, was a printer, author, scientist, philosopher, and statesman. An important figure during the founding of the United States, he signed both the Declaration of Independence and the U.S. Constitution. He established some of America's first libraries, hospitals, and colleges. Among his many inventions were the lightning rod, bifocal glasses, and a clock with three wheels to show hours, minutes, and seconds.

In 1732, he began an annual publication, *Poor Richard's Almanack*, which brought him great fame. Many of the sayings he wrote for the *Almanack* are still widely quoted today:

An apple a day keeps the doctor away.

Early to bed and early to rise, makes a man

       healthy, wealthy, and wise.

He that goes a-borrowing goes a-sorrowing.

Lost time is never found again.

If you would be loved, love and be lovable.

The doors of wisdom are never shut.

January–February: Chinese New Year

Based on the lunar calendar, the Chinese New Year falls between January 21 and February 19. The calendar follows a cycle of twelve years; each new year is named for one of twelve animals.

CHINESE LUNAR ZODIAC CALENDAR

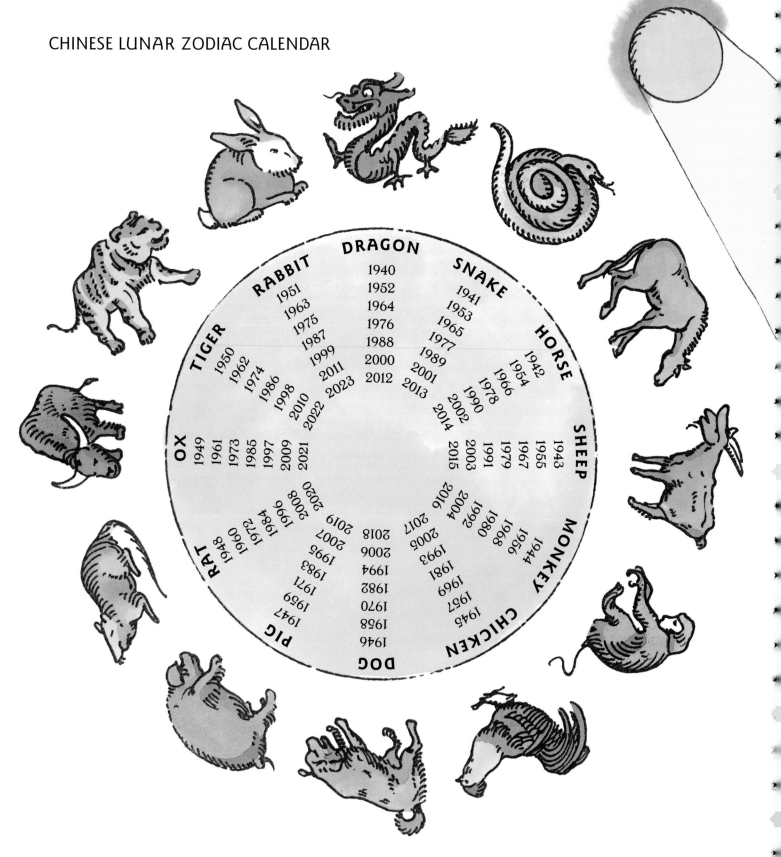

RABBIT
1951
1963
1975
1987
1999
2011
2023

DRAGON
1940
1952
1964
1976
1988
2000
2012

SNAKE
1941
1953
1965
1977
1989
2001
2013

TIGER
1950
1962
1974
1986
1998
2010
2022

HORSE
1942
1954
1966
1978
1990
2002
2014

OX
1949
1961
1973
1985
1997
2009
2021

SHEEP
1943
1955
1967
1979
1991
2003
2015

RAT
1948
1960
1972
1984
1996
2008
2020

MONKEY
1944
1956
1968
1980
1992
2004
2016

PIG
1947
1959
1971
1983
1995
2007
2019

CHICKEN
1945
1957
1969
1981
1993
2005
2017

DOG
1946
1958
1970
1982
1994
2006
2018

Prayer
for the Lunar
New Year

Janet S. Wong

This is the day
you grow another year wiser.

This is the day
you forget what you know to be impossible.

The moon loves to play a game.
Play.

Sweep your grudges out,
scatter them to nothing.

Scrub your wishes pure,
wash your heart clear.

Open your windows wide,
let the new year begin.

 February

African-American History Month
Presidents' Day: 3rd Monday

1
1902 Birth date: (James) Langston Hughes, poet, author

2 *Groundhog Day*

3 *Setsubun*
Japan's bean-throwing festival

1894 Birth date: Norman Rockwell, artist

4
1902 Birth date: Charles Augustus Lindbergh, aviator

1913 Birth date: Rosa Parks, civil rights leader

9
1773 Birth date: William Henry Harrison, 9th U.S. president

1870 U.S. Weather Service founded

10
1927 Birth date: Leontyne Price, opera singer

1950 Birth date: Mark Spitz, Olympic swimming champion

11
1847 Birth date: Thomas Alva Edison, inventor

1939 Birth date: Jane Yolen, author, poet

12
1809 Birth date: Abraham Lincoln, 16th U.S. president

17
1963 Birth date: Michael Jeffrey Jordan, basketball player

18
1930 Planet Pluto discovered by Clyde Tombaugh

1930 Elm Farm Ollie becomes the first cow to fly and be milked in an airplane

19
1878 Phonograph patented by Thomas Alva Edison

1984 Twin brothers make Olympic news when Phil Mahre wins the gold medal in slalom skiing and Steve Mahre wins the silver

2002 Vonetta Flowers becomes the first African-American to win an Olympic gold medal in bobsledding

20
1872 The largest museum in the United States, the Metropolitan Museum of Art, opens in New York, NY

25
1841 Birth date: Pierre Auguste Renoir, French artist

1870 Hiram Revels of Mississippi becomes the first African-American elected to the U.S. Senate

26
1829: Birth date: Levi Strauss, creator of the world's first pair of jeans—Levi's 501—for California gold miners in 1850

1919 Grand Canyon National Park in Arizona established

1985 Robert Penn Warren named the first U.S. poet laureate

27
1807: Birth date: Henry Wadsworth Longfellow, poet, author

1897: Birth date: Marian Anderson, opera singer

28
1940: Basketball game televised for the first time

Abraham Lincoln said:

"The ballot is stronger than the bullet."

February comes from the Latin Februarius. *The verb* februare *means "to purify."*

FLOWER: VIOLET

BIRTHSTONE: AMETHYST

ZODIAC SIGN: PISCES, THE FISH (FEBRUARY 19–MARCH 20)
PISCES ARE INSPIRED, COMPASSIONATE, CHARITABLE, AND, LIKE FISH, "GO WITH THE FLOW"!

5
1934 Birth date: Henry Louis ("Hank") Aaron, baseball player

1981 World's largest batch of Jell-O made in Brisbane, Australia: 7,700 gallons, costing $14,000

6
1788 Massachusetts: 6th state to enter the Union

1895 Birth date: George Herman ("Babe") Ruth, baseball player

1911 Birth date: Ronald Wilson Reagan, 40th U.S. president

7
1812 Birth date: Charles Dickens, English author

1827 Ballet introduced in U.S. by French danseuse Mme. Francisquy Hutin

1867 Birth date: Laura Ingalls Wilder, author of the *Little House* series

8
1828 Birth date: Jules Verne, French author

13
1892 Birth date: Grant Wood, artist

1923 Birth date: Charles Elwood ("Chuck") Yeager, aviator who broke the sound barrier for the first time on October 14, 1947

14 *Valentine's Day*
1859 Birth date: George Washington Gale Ferris, engineer, inventor of the Ferris wheel

1859 Oregon: 33rd state to enter the Union

1912 Arizona: 48th state to enter the Union

15
1564 Birth date: Galileo Galilei, Italian astronomer

1820 Birth date: Susan Brownell Anthony, women's rights activist

16
1908 Birth date: Mary Le Duc O'Neill, poet

21
1828 *Cherokee Phoenix* becomes the first Native American newspaper published in both English and Cherokee and appears until 1935

1885 Washington Monument in Washington, D.C., dedicated to honor George Washington, 1st U.S. president

1893 Birth date: Andrés Segovia, Spanish guitarist

22
1732 Birth date: George Washington, 1st U.S. president

1892 Birth date: Edna St. Vincent Millay, poet

1918 Birth date: Robert Pershing Wadlow, recorded as the tallest man in the world; 8 feet 11.1 inches tall

23
1685 Birth date: George Frideric Handel, English composer

1868 Birth date: William Edward Burghardt ("W. E. B.") Du Bois, educator

1874 Game of lawn tennis patented by Maj. Walter Clapton Wingfield

24
1786 Birth date: Wilhelm Carl Grimm, German collector of fairy tales

29 *Leap Year Day*
1792 Birth date: Gioacchino Antonio Rossini, Italian composer

1940 Hattie McDaniel becomes the first African-American to win an Academy Award, for her role in *Gone with the Wind*

WEATHER REPORT
On February 6, 1978, a massive nor'easter buried cities in the northeastern United States, with 25 to 30 inches falling in Boston, Massachusetts; 18 inches in New York, New York; 16 inches in Philadelphia, Pennsylvania; and 14 inches in Baltimore, Maryland.

My People

Langston Hughes

The night is beautiful,
So the faces of my people.

The stars are beautiful,
So the eyes of my people.

Beautiful, also, is the sun.
Beautiful, also, are the souls of my people.

February 1: Birth date: (James) Langston Hughes (1902–1967)

Hughes, born in Joplin, Missouri, published his first poem, "The Negro Speaks of Rivers," in 1921. He went on to write plays, nonfiction books, novels, short stories, operettas, and newspaper columns.

His poetry earned him the title America's Black Poet Laureate. In 2002, on the 100th celebration of his birth date, the United States issued a commemorative postage stamp in his honor.

February 2: Groundhog Day

In the small town of Punxsutawney, Pennsylvania, a groundhog, "Punxsutawney Phil," predicts when spring will officially come. If he sees his shadow, he goes back into his hole for six more weeks of winter.

Groundhog

Maria Fleming

People shoo me
from their lawn,
scold me,
chase me,
want me gone,
treat me like
some kind of pest,
a most unwelcome
garden guest.

Then one day,
for mysterious reasons,
they crown me—

ME!—

King of Seasons.

Will spring come soon?
Will winter flee?
The world awaits
my royal decree.

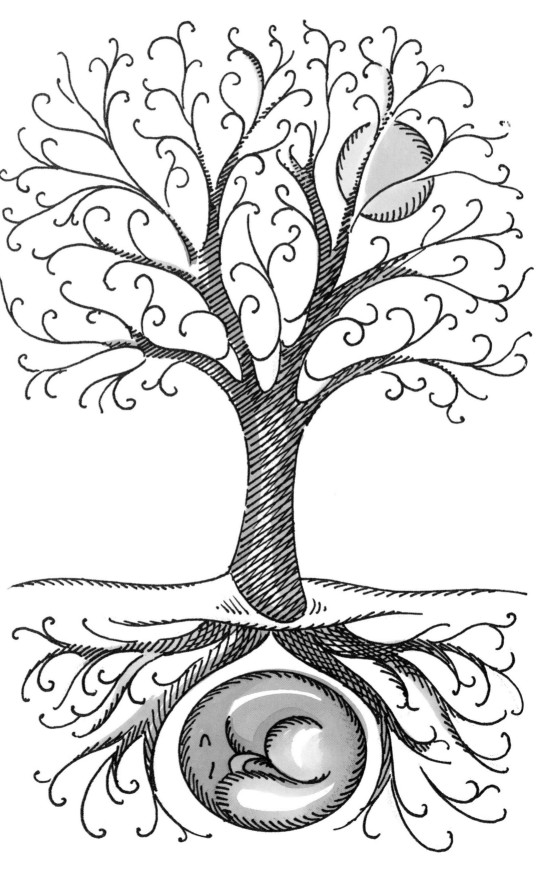

19

February 4: Birth date: Charles Augustus Lindbergh (1902–1974)

Born in Detroit, Michigan, "Lucky Lindy" made the first solo nonstop flight across the Atlantic Ocean from Roosevelt Field, Long Island, New York, to Paris, France, on May 20–21, 1927. The trip took 33.5 hours.

Flying-Man *Mother Goose*

Flying-man, Flying-man,
Up in the sky,
Where are you going to
Flying so high?

Over the mountains
And over the sea,
Flying-man, Flying-man
Can't you take me?

February 9, 1870: U.S. Weather Service founded

Weather *Anonymous*

Whether the weather be fine,
Or whether the weather be not,
Whether the weather be cold,
Or whether the weather be hot,
We'll weather the weather
Whatever the weather
Whether we like it or not.

February 14: Valentine's Day

The origins of Valentine's Day can be traced back to the ancient Roman celebration Lupercalia, a holiday for lovers. Today it is one of the most widely observed unofficial holidays.

Each year thousands of cards are mailed to the postmaster at Valentines, Virginia, for a Valentine postmark.

It is a day to express love, especially through poetry.

I Love You

Anonymous

I love you,

I love you,

I love you divine,

Please give me your bubble gum,

You're sitting on mine!

February 27: Birth date:
Henry Wadsworth Longfellow (1807–1882)

Born in Portland, Maine, Longfellow became the first American poet inducted into the Poet's Corner in Westminster Abbey, London, England. Known for such long narrative poems as *The Song of Hiawatha* and *Paul Revere's Ride,* he also created verse that became popular for children to recite, such as "The Village Blacksmith" and:

From
The Rainy Day
Henry Wadsworth Longfellow

The day is cold, and dark, and dreary;

It rains, and the wind is never weary;

The vine still clings to the mouldering wall,

But at every gust the dead leaves fall

    And the day is dark and dreary. . . .

Be still, sad heart! and cease repining;

Behind the clouds is the sun still shining;

Thy fate is the common fate of all,

Into each life some rain must fall,

    Some days must be dark and dreary.

February 27: Birth date: Marian Anderson (1897–1993)

Born in Philadelphia, Pennsylvania, Anderson began singing in church choirs at the age of six.

In 1939, having been banned by the Daughters of the American Revolution from performing onstage at Constitution Hall in Washington, D.C., because of her color, she gave an outdoor concert at the Lincoln Memorial on a cold Easter Sunday, April 9, before seventy-five thousand supporters.

Anderson went on to become the first African-American to be named a permanent member of the Metropolitan Opera Company in New York, New York (1955), and the first African-American to perform in the White House. In 1958, she was an alternate delegate to the United Nations.

Remembering Marian Anderson

Joyce Carol Thomas

The regal woman pulled her thick coat close and
Stood on the stony steps of the Lincoln Memorial
Where an army of Washer Women in
Sunday-go-to-meeting, head-warming hats
Gazed up at her with hope and admiration

Marian Anderson breathed deeply
Closed her eyes
And looked down the corridors of history
Until she touched
The textures of the future
Compassion, fairness, democracy

A top note, that's what I need, she thought

She opened her mouth
And threw the first note into the corner of the sky
Hearing it, freedom stirred
And Marian Anderson began
Singing the conscience of a people

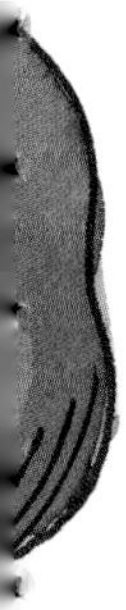

My country 'tis of thee
Sweet land of liberty
Of thee we sing

And all the Colored folks
Who died in foreign lands and on home soil
Paraded across memory
While people of goodwill wiped away the tears
Streaming down their cheeks like April rain

Grown-ups marveled at the honesty in her song
At the way it opened closed minds
At the way it reminded them
Of what they had always known

Children heard in the pure tones
The vibrant call of
A determined spirit
And the strong blood ran throbbing
Through the veins of their lives

Here we sit
Here we stand today,
Marian Anderson
Victorious in our own little
Corners of courage
Chanting the noble colors you sang
With pride
With stamina
With vision

*M*arch

1 **1803** Ohio: 17th state to enter the Union **1867** Nebraska: 37th state to enter the Union **1921** Birth date: Richard Purdy Wilbur, poet **1967** Lap belts become mandatory car equipment in the U.S.	**2** **1793** Birth date: Samuel Houston, frontiersman, Texas political leader **1904** Birth date: Theodor Seuss ("Dr. Seuss") Geisel, author, illustrator	**3** *Hina Matsuri* Japanese doll festival **1845** Florida: 27th state to enter the Union **1847** Birth date: Alexander Graham Bell, inventor of the telephone	**4** **1678** Birth date: Antonio Vivaldi, Italian composer **1791** Vermont: 14th state to enter the Union
9 **1454** Birth date: Amerigo Vespucci, Italian explorer	**10** **1913** Death of Harriet Tubman, abolitionist	**11** **1893** Birth date: Wanda Hazel Gág, author-illustrator of *Millions of Cats*	**12** **1890** Birth date: Vaslav Nijinsky, Russian ballet dancer **1952** Birth date: Naomi Shihab Nye, poet, author
17 *St. Patrick's Day* **1909** Birth date: Lilian Moore, poet	**18** **1837** Birth date: Grover Cleveland, 22nd and 24th U.S. president **1950** Birth date: Douglas Florian, poet, illustrator	**19** *Swallow Day* Each year swallows return to Mission San Juan Capistrano, California, from their winter home in Goya, Argentina	**20** **1926** Birth date: Mitsumasa Anno, Japanese author, illustrator **1928** Birth date: Fred Rogers ("Mr. Rogers"), television star of *Mister Rogers' Neighborhood*
25 **1881** Birth date: Béla Bartók, Hungarian composer, pianist	**26** **1874** Birth date: Robert Lee Frost, poet **1930** Birth date: Sandra Day O'Connor, first woman to serve on the U.S. Supreme Court	**27** **1845** Birth date: Wilhelm Konrad Roentgen, German inventor of the X-ray **1955** First coast-to-coast color television broadcast transmitted	**28** **1797** Washing machine patented by Nathaniel Briggs

Albert Einstein said:

"Imagination is more important than knowledge."

26

Named for the Roman god of war, Mars, March was the first month of the Roman calendar until the adoption of the Julian calendar in 46 B.C.

FLOWER: DAFFODIL
BIRTHSTONE: BLOODSTONE
ZODIAC SIGN: ARIES, THE RAM (MARCH 21–APRIL 20)
ARIANS ARE ENERGETIC, DYNAMIC, AND INDEPENDENT. THEY LOVE TO GET THINGS STARTED, AND THEY MAKE SURE THINGS HAPPEN.

5
1853 Birth date: Howard Pyle, illustrator, author of *The Merry Adventures of Robin Hood*

6
1475 Birth date: Michelangelo Buonarroti, Italian artist

1806 Birth date: Elizabeth Barrett Browning, English poet

1972 Birth date: Shaquille Rashaun ("Shaq") O'Neal, basketball player

7
1849 Birth date: Luther Burbank, horticulturist

1886 Telephone patented by Alexander Graham Bell

1933 Charles Darrow invents Monopoly

8
1859 Birth date: Kenneth Grahame, Scottish author of *The Wind in the Willows*

13
1781 Planet Uranus discovered by Sir William Herschel

1877 Earmuffs patented by Chester Greenwood

14
1804 Birth date: Johann Strauss, Austrian composer

1879 Birth date: Albert Einstein, physicist

15
1767 Birth date: Andrew Jackson, 7th U.S. president

1820 Maine: 23rd state to enter the Union

16
1751 Birth date: James Madison, 4th U.S. president

21 *First day of spring*
1685 Birth date: Johann Sebastian Bach, German composer

22 *Puerto Rico Emancipation Day*
Commemoration of end of slavery in 1873

1846 Birth date: Randolph Caldecott, English artist

1941 Birth date: Billy Collins, eleventh U.S. poet laureate

1960 Laser (light amplification by stimulated emission of radiation) patented by Arthur Schawlow and Charles Townes

23
1857 Elisha Graves Otis installs the first passenger elevator

24
1874 Birth date: Erich Weiss ("Harry Houdini"), world's greatest escape artist

1919 Birth date: Lawrence Ferlinghetti, poet

2002 Halle Berry becomes the first African-American woman to win an Academy Award for Best Actress

29
1790 Birth date: John Tyler, 10th U.S. president

30
1746 Birth date: Francisco José de Goya y Lucientes, Spanish artist

1820 Birth date: Anna Sewell, English author of *Black Beauty*

1853 Birth date: Vincent van Gogh, Dutch artist

1858 Pencil with attached eraser patented by Hyman L. Lipman

31
1732 Birth date: Franz Joseph Haydn, Austrian composer

1927 Birth date: César Estrada Chávez, union organizer

WEATHER REPORT

On March 29, 1945, the temperature in Providence, Rhode Island, soared to 90 degrees, establishing a March record for the New England area.

March 10, 1913: Death of Harriet Tubman

Araminta Ross (1820?–1913), later known as Harriet Tubman, was born into slavery in Dorchester County, Maryland. Escaping from her master, she became a "conductor" on the Underground Railroad, a system to help slaves reach freedom. During the Civil War, she led more than three hundred African-Americans from slavery, earning her the nickname Black Moses.

The date of Tubman's birth is unknown. She died in Auburn, New York. In 1978, a U.S. commemorative stamp, designed by Jerry Pinkney, was issued to honor her courageous achievements.

Freedom!

Harriet Tubman
Auburn, New York, 1861

Bobbi Katz

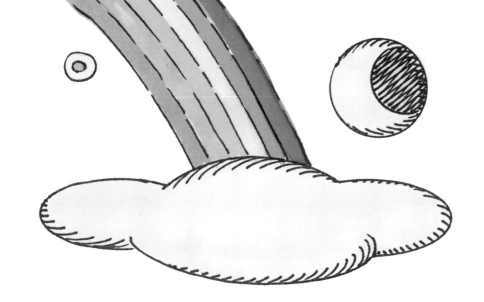

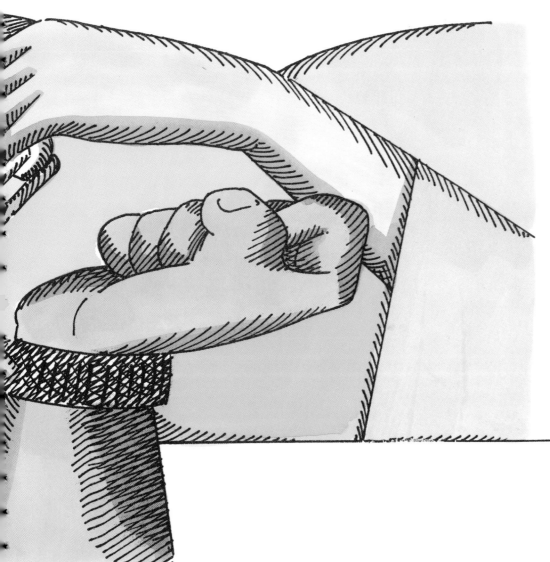

Before I rode "The Railroad,"
    I didn't understand.
I thought that tracks were tunneled
    underneath the land.
The Underground Railroad
    runs out of sight.
The last stop is freedom
    if you ride it right.
Good people gave me food
    and hid me all the way,
until I reached Pennsylvania
    at sunrise one day.
I stared at these black hands
    to make sure I was me.
I felt I was in heaven.
    At last I was free!

I worked as a cook,
    saved my money
        and then . . .
    I went down South
    again and . . . again
to lead others to the stations:
    women, children, men.
Yes, I worked and I saved
    and I kept going back.
I never lost a passenger
    or ran my train off the track.

Folks began to call me Moses.
    The thought tickled me.
Moses! There was a conductor
    who set God's children free.

March 17: St. Patrick's Day

Patrick, the patron saint of Ireland, was not Irish. He was born about A.D. 385 somewhere in western England. St. Patrick's Day commemorates his death on March 17 (the year is uncertain; estimates range from 461 to 464). The first St. Patrick's Day celebration in the United States was held in Boston, Massachusetts, in 1737.

For centuries the shamrock, a small, green, three-leaved plant resembling clover, has been an emblem of Ireland. Folklore tells us that when St. Patrick drove the snakes out of Ireland, he stood in a shamrock patch. Part of an old Irish song gives St. Patrick credit for bringing the plant to Ireland.

There's a dear little plant
    that grows in our Isle
'Twas St. Patrick himself
    sure that set it.
And the sun on his labor
    with pleasure did smile,
And with dew from his eye
    oft-times wet it.
It grows through the bog,
    through the brake,
    through the mireland,
And he called it the dear
    little shamrock of Ireland.

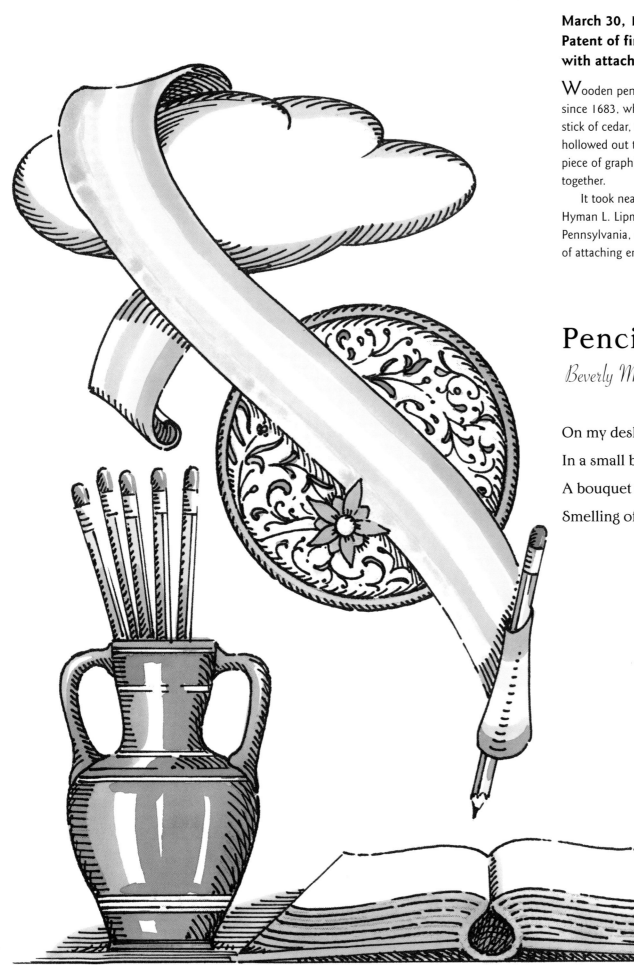

March 30, 1858:
Patent of first pencil
with attached eraser

Wooden pencils have been around since 1683, when J. Pettus took a small stick of cedar, slit it down the middle, hollowed out the center, inserted a piece of graphite, and glued it all together.

It took nearly 200 years before Hyman L. Lipman from Philadelphia, Pennsylvania, came up with the idea of attaching erasers to them.

Pencils
Beverly McLoughland

On my desk
In a small brown vase,
A bouquet of tall yellow flowers
Smelling of cedar.

National Poetry Month

Young People's Poetry Week: 3rd week of National Poetry Month

Arbor Day: Last Friday in most states, but date varies

Birthday of the Buddha: April or May, based on the lunar calendar; celebrates the founder of Buddhism, Siddhartha Gautama

1 *April Fools' Day*

1873 Birth date: Sergei Vasilievich Rachmaninov, Russian composer, pianist

2

1805 Birth date: Hans Christian Andersen, Danish author of *Fairy Tales*

1834 Birth date: Frédéric Auguste Bartholdi, French sculptor, creator of the Statue of Liberty

3

1783 Birth date: Washington Irving, author of "Rip Van Winkle"

4

1887 Susanna Medora Salter is the first woman elected mayor of an American community, Argonia, KS

9

1898 Birth date: Paul Bustill Robeson, football player, actor, singer

10

1847 Birth date: Joseph Pulitzer, journalist, founder of the Pulitzer prizes

1849 Safety pin patented by Walter Hunt

1872 First Arbor Day celebration

1897 Birth date: Eric Mowbray Knight, author of *Lassie Come-Home*

11

1968 U.S. Civil Rights Act becomes law

12

1961 Yuri Gagarin, Soviet cosmonaut, becomes the first human in space

17

1897 Birth date: Thornton Niven Wilder, author, playwright

18

1934 The first Laundromat, called a *washeteria*, opens in Fort Worth, TX

1987 Richard Purdy Wilbur named America's second poet laureate

19

1775 Start of the American Revolution as British fired "the shot heard round the world"

20

1979 35 riders pedal the longest bicycle ever built, 66 feet 11 inches long

25

1874 Birth date: Guglielmo Marconi, Italian inventor

1901 First license plates for automobiles issued, New York, NY

26

1785 Birth date: John James Audubon, ornithologist, painter of birdlife

27

1822 Birth date: Ulysses Simpson Grant, 18th U.S. president

1927 Birth date: Coretta Scott King, civil rights leader, author, lecturer

28

1758 Birth date: James Monroe, 5th U.S. president

1788 Maryland: 7th state to enter the Union

1925 Birth date: Barbara Juster Esbensen, poet

William Shakespeare said:

"All the world's a stage,
And all the men and women merely players. . . ." —From *As You Like It*

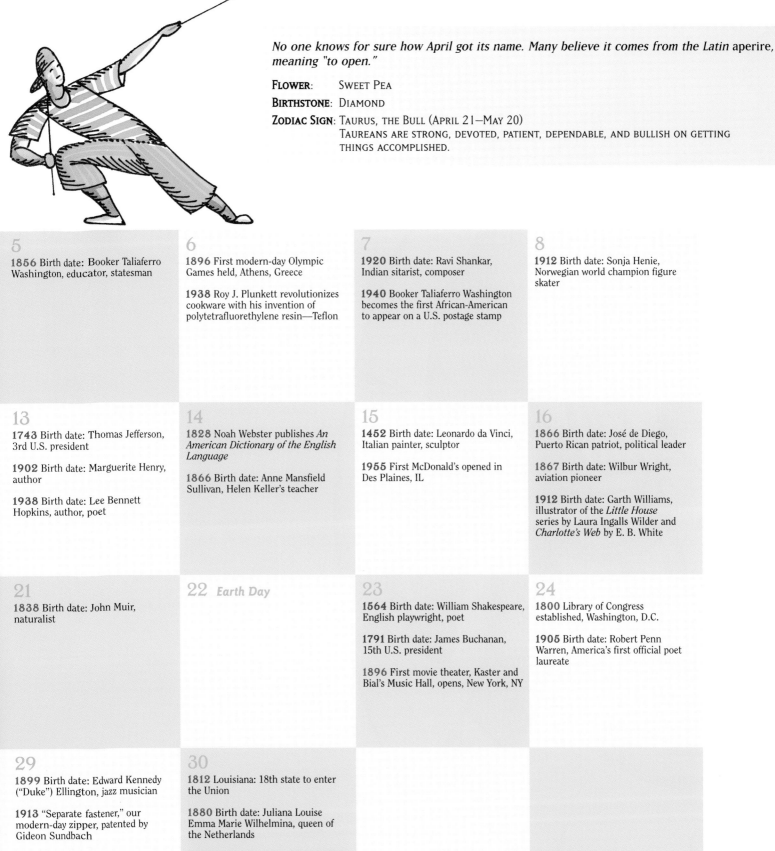

No one knows for sure how April got its name. Many believe it comes from the Latin aperire, *meaning "to open."*

FLOWER: SWEET PEA

BIRTHSTONE: DIAMOND

ZODIAC SIGN: TAURUS, THE BULL (APRIL 21—MAY 20)
TAUREANS ARE STRONG, DEVOTED, PATIENT, DEPENDABLE, AND BULLISH ON GETTING THINGS ACCOMPLISHED.

5

1856 Birth date: Booker Taliaferro Washington, educator, statesman

6

1896 First modern-day Olympic Games held, Athens, Greece

1938 Roy J. Plunkett revolutionizes cookware with his invention of polytetrafluoroethylene resin—Teflon

7

1920 Birth date: Ravi Shankar, Indian sitarist, composer

1940 Booker Taliaferro Washington becomes the first African-American to appear on a U.S. postage stamp

8

1912 Birth date: Sonja Henie, Norwegian world champion figure skater

13

1743 Birth date: Thomas Jefferson, 3rd U.S. president

1902 Birth date: Marguerite Henry, author

1938 Birth date: Lee Bennett Hopkins, author, poet

14

1828 Noah Webster publishes *An American Dictionary of the English Language*

1866 Birth date: Anne Mansfield Sullivan, Helen Keller's teacher

15

1452 Birth date: Leonardo da Vinci, Italian painter, sculptor

1955 First McDonald's opened in Des Plaines, IL

16

1866 Birth date: José de Diego, Puerto Rican patriot, political leader

1867 Birth date: Wilbur Wright, aviation pioneer

1912 Birth date: Garth Williams, illustrator of the *Little House* series by Laura Ingalls Wilder and *Charlotte's Web* by E. B. White

21

1838 Birth date: John Muir, naturalist

22 *Earth Day*

23

1564 Birth date: William Shakespeare, English playwright, poet

1791 Birth date: James Buchanan, 15th U.S. president

1896 First movie theater, Kaster and Bial's Music Hall, opens, New York, NY

24

1800 Library of Congress established, Washington, D.C.

1905 Birth date: Robert Penn Warren, America's first official poet laureate

29

1899 Birth date: Edward Kennedy ("Duke") Ellington, jazz musician

1913 "Separate fastener," our modern-day zipper, patented by Gideon Sundbach

30

1812 Louisiana: 18th state to enter the Union

1880 Birth date: Juliana Louise Emma Marie Wilhelmina, queen of the Netherlands

1988 Largest banana split, created in Selinsgrove, PA, measures 4.55 miles

WEATHER REPORT

On April 12, 1934, the highest-velocity natural wind ever recorded on the earth's surface occurred at the Mount Washington Observatory in New Hampshire, with gusts reaching 231 miles per hour.

April I: April Fools' Day

It is not known when April Fools' Day began, but today it is celebrated in many countries. The French call it *poisson d'avril*, and try to pin a paper *poisson*, or fish, on someone's back without getting caught. It is called Huntigowk Day in Scotland, where people are sent out to hunt the *gowk*, a cuckoo bird.

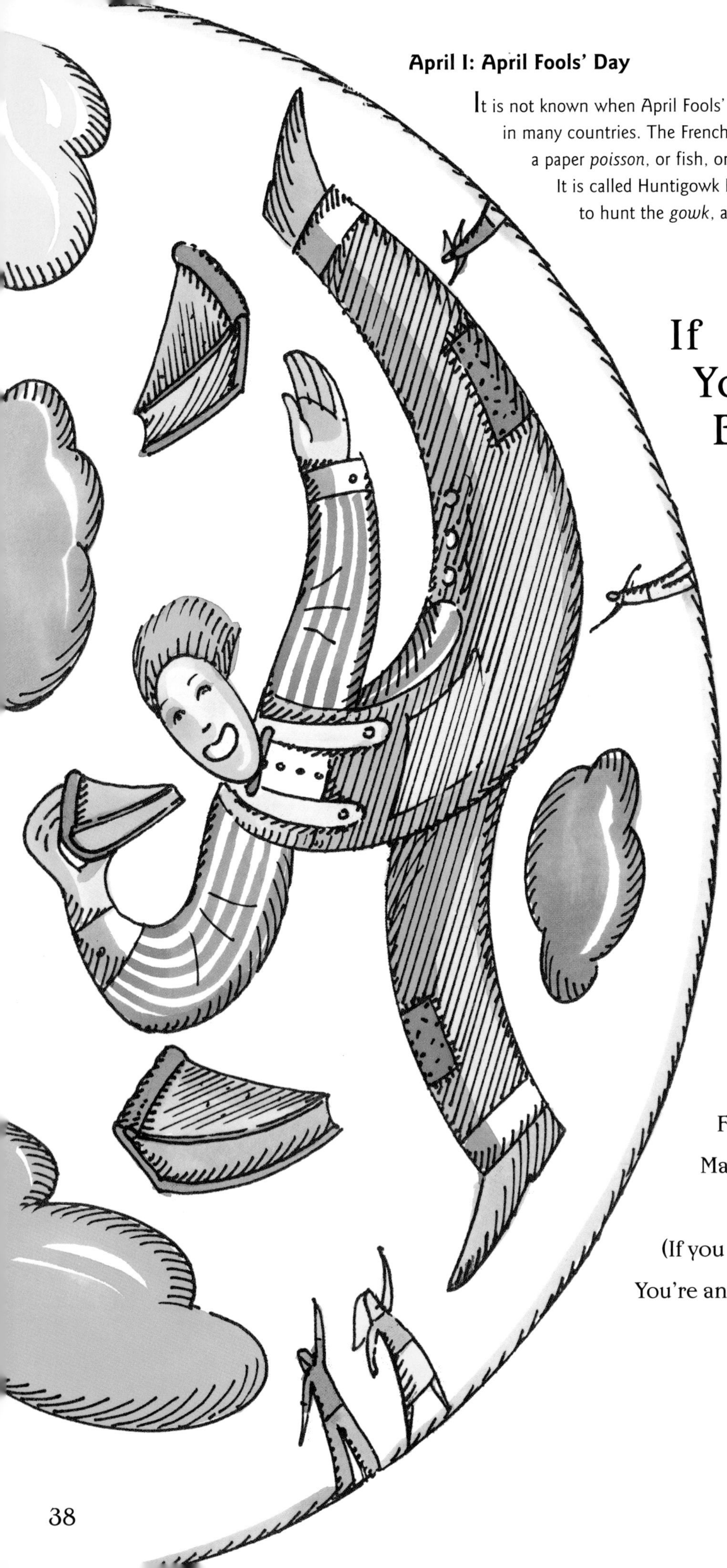

If
You
Believe
Me

Lee Bennett Hopkins

Lenny, sailing down the river,
Ate tons and tons of fresh-ground liver.

Peter, flying in the sky,
Ate gobs and gobs of pigsty pie.

Heather, sitting up in bed,
Ate chunks and chunks of codfish head.

Mickey, riding a caboose,
Ate slabs and slabs of uncooked moose.

Foods *so* tasty
Made them drool—

(If you believe me—
You're an

APRIL FOOL!)

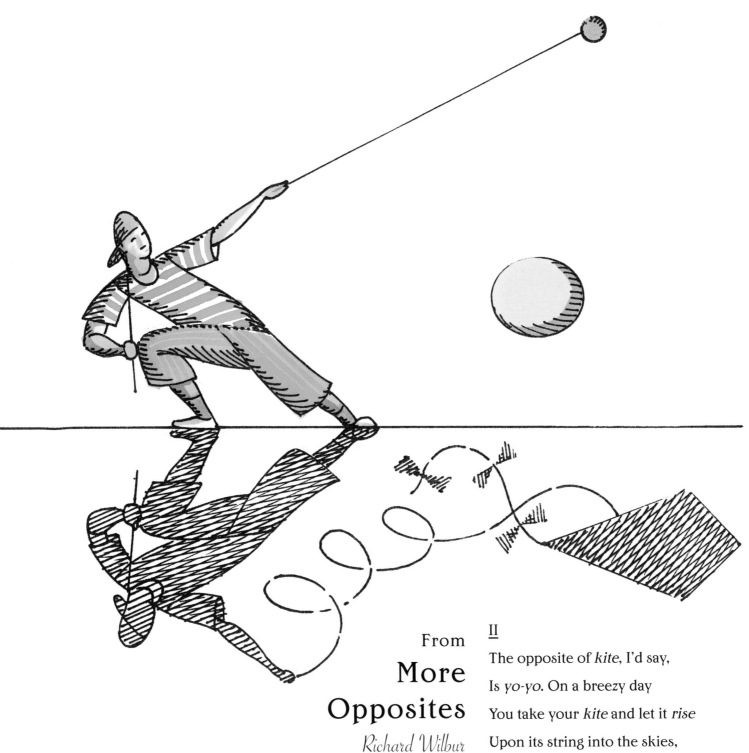

From

More Opposites

Richard Wilbur

April 18, 1987: Richard Purdy Wilbur named America's second poet laureate

Born in New York, New York, two-time Pulitzer Prize winner and U. S. poet laureate Wilbur has created books of poetry for adults and children since 1947. He is also known for writing the libretto, with playwright Lillian Hellman, for the musical version of Voltaire's *Candide*.

II

The opposite of *kite*, I'd say,

Is *yo-yo*. On a breezy day

You take your *kite* and let it *rise*

Upon its string into the skies,

And then you pull it *down* with ease

(Unless it crashes in the trees).

A *yo-yo*, though, drops *down*, and then

You quickly bring it *up* again

By pulling deftly on its string

(If you can work the blasted thing).

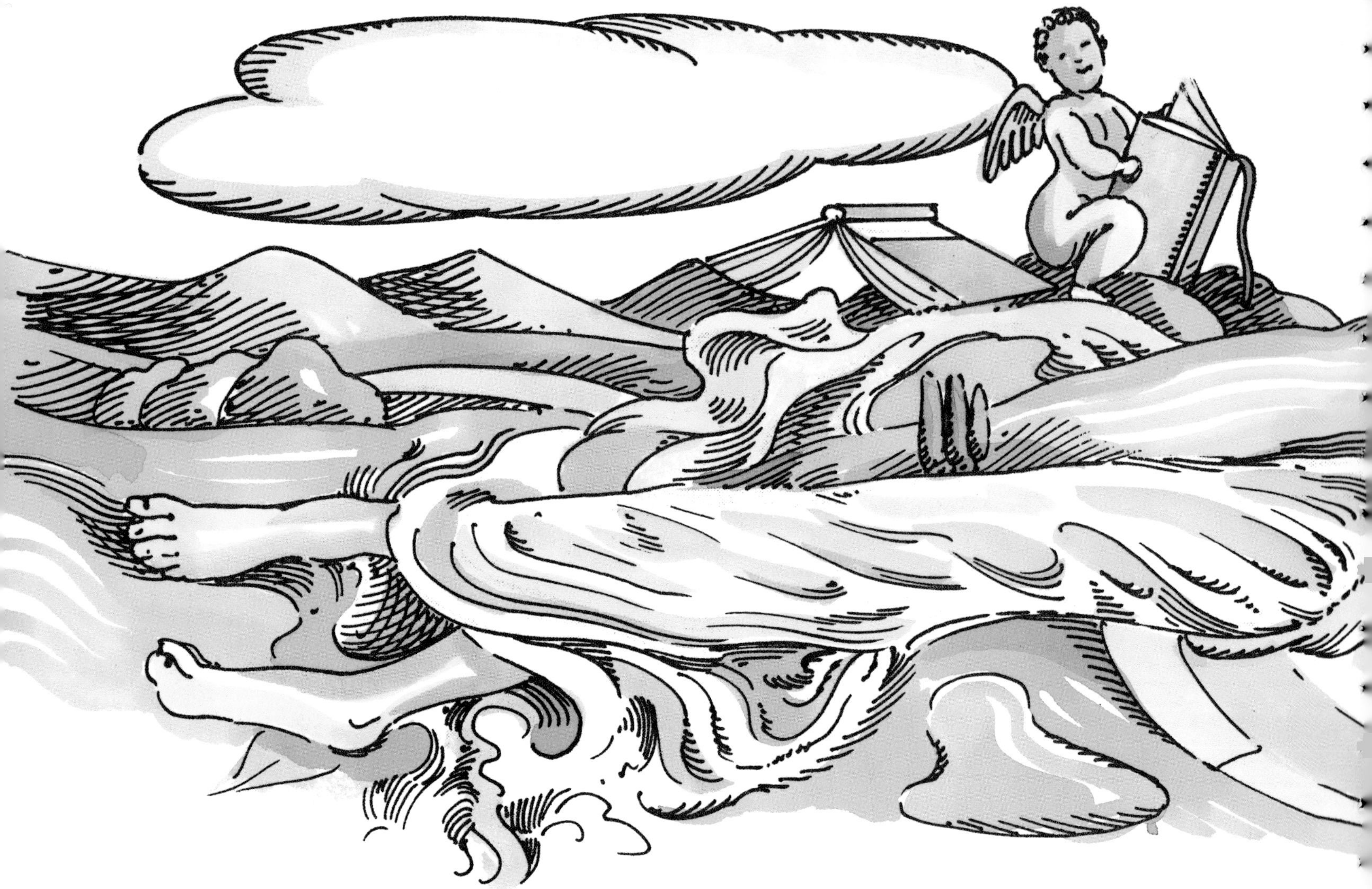

Earth, What Will You Give Me?

Beverly McLoughland

Earth, what will you give me
In summer,
In summer,
Earth, what will you give me
In summer
Serene?

I'll give you my fields
Made of lilies,
Of lilies,
I'll give you my fields
Made of lilies
And green.

April 22: Earth Day

The first Earth Day was sparked in 1970 by Senator Gaylord Nelson of Wisconsin to help clean the earth. Over 20 million Americans took part. Two decades later, on April 22, 1990, 200 million people in more than 140 countries celebrated the second Earth Day, which is now an annual event.

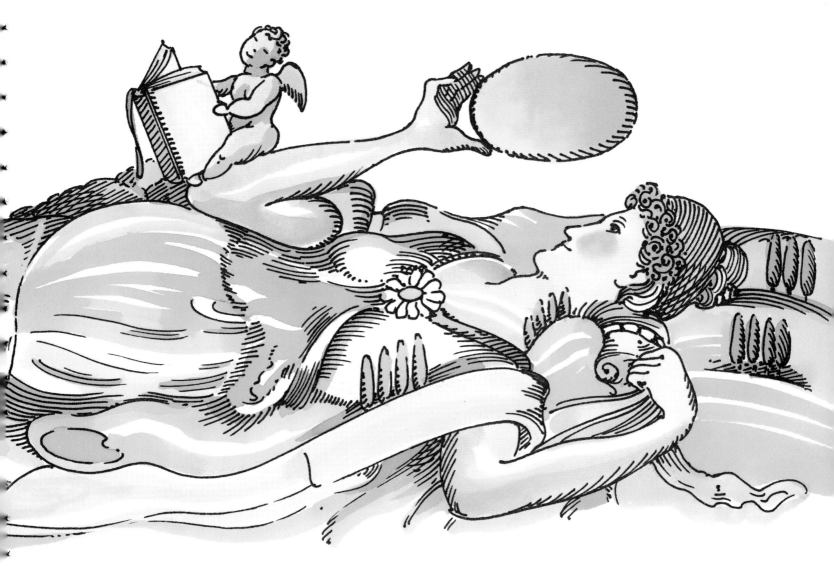

And what will you give me
In autumn,
In autumn,
And what will you give me
In autumn
So bold?

I'll give you my leaves
Made of maple,
Of maple,
I'll give you my leaves
Made of maple
And gold.

And what will you give me
In winter,
In winter,
And what will you give me
In winter
So light?

I'll give you my stars
Made of crystal,
Of crystal,
I'll give you my stars
Made of crystal
And white.

And what will you give me
In springtime,
In springtime,
And what will you give me
In springtime
So new?

I'll give you my nests
Made of grasses,
Of grasses,
I'll give you my nests
Made of grasses
And blue.

41

April 26: Birth date: John James Audubon (1785–1851)

Born in Les Cayes, Santo Domingo (now Haiti), Audubon came to the United States in 1803. As a teenager he began extensive observations of birds. His lifelong interest led to the publication of *Birds of America*, featuring drawings and paintings that remain one of the greatest achievements in ornithology.

Little Birds *Anonymous*

Little birds sit in their nest and beg,

All mouth that once had been all egg.

National Poetry Month: Young People's Poetry Week

Young People's Poetry Week, celebrated the third week in April, has been an important part of National Poetry Month since 1999. It is a time for everyone to read, write, and enjoy poetry. About poetry, poets have said:

"If I read a book and it makes my whole body so cold that no fire can ever warm me, I know that is poetry."—Emily Dickinson

"A poem . . . begins as a lump in the throat, a sense of wrong, a homesickness, a lovesickness."—Robert Frost

"Poetry is a record of the best and happiest moments for the happiest of minds."
—Percy Bysshe Shelley

"Poetry is cries and laughter from the heart."
—Joyce Carol Thomas

May

Mother's Day: 2nd Sunday

Memorial Day: 4th Monday

1 *May Day*
Mother Goose Day

1931 Empire State Building dedicated, New York, NY

2

1903? Birth date: Harry Lillis ("Bing") Crosby, actor, singer

1933 Birth date: Bobbi Katz, poet

1987 Largest game of Twister, played by 4,160 people at the University of Massachusetts

3

1898 Birth date: Golda Meir, Israeli prime minister

4

1989 Space shuttle *Atlantis* blasts off from Cape Canaveral, FL, launching the Magellan space probe to map Venus surface

9

1860 Birth date: Sir James Matthew Barrie, Scottish author of *Peter Pan*

1914 Mother's Day becomes a holiday

10

1930 Adler Planetarium, the first American public planetarium, opens in Chicago, IL

11

1858 Minnesota: 32nd state to enter the Union

1888 Birth date: Irving Berlin, songwriter, lyricist of over 1,000 songs, including "God Bless America"

1894 Birth date: Martha Graham, dancer

12

1812 Birth date: Edward Lear, English poet

1820 Birth date: Florence Nightingale, English founder of modern nursing

17

1749 Birth date: Edward Jenner, English physician; discovered scientific basis of vaccination

1929 Birth date: Eloise Greenfield, poet

2000 Dinosaur named Sue exhibited at Field Museum, Chicago, IL

18

1919 Birth date: Margot Fonteyn, English ballerina

1920 Birth date: Pope John Paul II (Karol Wojtyla), first non-Italian to be elected pope in 456 years and first Polish pope

19

1925 Birth date: Malcolm Little ("Malcolm X"), civil rights leader

20

1932 Amelia Earhart becomes the first woman to fly solo across the Atlantic

25

1803 Birth date: Ralph Waldo Emerson, author, poet

1878 Birth date: Bill ("Bojangles") Robinson, tap dancer

1908 Birth date: Theodore Roethke, poet

1938 Birth date: Joyce Carol Thomas, poet

2001 Erik Weihenmeyer becomes the first blind person to reach the summit of Mount Everest

26

1951 Birth date: Sally Kristen Ride, first American woman in space

27

1819 Birth date: Julia Ward Howe, lyricist, "Battle Hymn of the Republic"

1930 Adhesive tape, later manufactured as Scotch tape, patented by Richard Gurley Drew

1937 Golden Gate Bridge opens in California

28

1888 Birth date: James Francis ("Jim") Thorpe, Olympic champion

Ralph Waldo Emerson said:

"Insist on yourself; never imitate."

The name for May has a mixed history. Some say it stems from Maia, the goddess of growth, while others maintain the month was named to pay tribute to the Majores, or Maiores, the older branch of the Roman Senate. The number of days has varied from twenty-two to thirty to today's thirty-one.

FLOWER: LILY OF THE VALLEY
BIRTHSTONE: EMERALD
ZODIAC SIGN: GEMINI, THE TWINS (MAY 21–JUNE 21)
GEMINIS ARE CURIOUS, CLEVER, AND CAPABLE OF TACKLING MANY THINGS AT ONCE.

5 *Cinco de Mayo*
Mexican celebration of defeat of a French invasion, 1862

1921 Birth date: Arthur Leonard Schawlow, physicist, coinventor of laser beams

1942 Birth date: J. Patrick Lewis, poet

6
1931 Birth date: Willie Howard Mays, Jr., baseball player

1954 Birth date: Kristine O'Connell George, poet

7
1812 Birth date: Robert Browning, English poet

1833 Birth date: Johannes Brahms, German composer

1840 Birth date: Pyotr ("Peter") Ilych Tchaikovsky, Russian composer

1861 Birth date: Sir Rabindranath Tagore, Indian poet, author, Nobel Peace Prize winner

8
1884 Birth date: Harry S. Truman, 33rd U.S. president

13
1864 First soldier buried in Arlington National Cemetery, VA

14
1948 Israel becomes an independent state

15
1856 Birth date: Lyman ("L.") Frank Baum, author of *Oz* books

1930 Ellen Church becomes the first flight attendant; her United Airlines trip was from San Francisco, CA, to Cheyenne, WY

16
1804 Birth date: Elizabeth Palmer Peabody, educator; opened the first American kindergarten in 1860, Boston, MA

1975 Junko Tabei, Japanese mountaineer, becomes the first woman climber to reach the peak of Mount Everest

21
1881 American Red Cross originates with Clara Barton as president

22
1844 Birth date: Mary Stevenson Cassatt, artist

1892 Dr. W. Sheffield invents toothpaste tube

23
1788 South Carolina: 8th state to enter the Union

1910 Birth date: Margaret Wise Brown, author

24
1883 Brooklyn Bridge opens in New York, NY

29
1736 Birth date: Patrick Henry, colonial leader

1790 Rhode Island: 13th state to enter the Union

1848 Wisconsin: 30th state to enter the Union

1917 Birth date: John Fitzgerald Kennedy, 35th U.S. president

30
1783 *Pennsylvania Evening Post* becomes the first daily newspaper published in the U.S., by Benjamin Towne in Philadelphia

1868 Memorial Day first observed

1903 Birth date: Countee Cullen, poet

1922 Lincoln Memorial in Washington, D.C., dedicated to honor Abraham Lincoln, 16th U.S. president

31
1819 Birth date: Walter ("Walt") Whitman, poet

WEATHER REPORT
On May 17, 1979, the temperature dipped to 12 degrees at the Mauna Kea Observatory, establishing an all-time record low for Hawaii.

May 9, 1914: Mother's Day first observed

In 1872, Julia Ward Howe, lyricist of "The Battle Hymn of the Republic," suggested Mother's Day as a day of peace in the United States. In 1907, Anna Jarvis, from Philadelphia, Pennsylvania, led a campaign for a nationwide observance. The holiday did not receive official recognition until May 9, 1914, when President Woodrow Wilson signed a resolution proclaiming Mother's Day an annual observance.

Many countries throughout the world celebrate Mother's Day at different times.

Mother to Son
Langston Hughes

Well, son, I'll tell you:

Life for me ain't been no crystal stair.

It's had tacks in it,

And splinters,

And boards torn up,

And places with no carpet on the floor—

Bare.

But all the time

I'se been a-climbin' on,

And reachin' landin's,

And turnin' corners,

And sometimes goin' in the dark

Where there ain't been no light.

So boy, don't you turn back.

Don't you set down on the steps

'Cause you finds it kinder hard.

Don't you fall now—

For I'se still goin' honey,

I'se still climbin',

And life for me ain't been no crystal stair.

May 12: Birth date: Edward Lear (1812–1888)

"If I write nonsense I am pervaded by smiles," Lear told a friend. And what nonsense he created! Besides his classics, "The Quangle Wangle's Hat" and "The Owl and the Pussycat," he is also known for his Lear-ickle limericks:

There was a young lady of Firle,

Whose hair was addicted to curl;

    It curled up a tree,

    And all over the sea,

That expansive young lady of Firle.

There was an Old Man with a beard,

Who said, "It is just as I feared!

    Two owls and a hen,

    Four larks and a wren

Have all built their nests in my beard!"

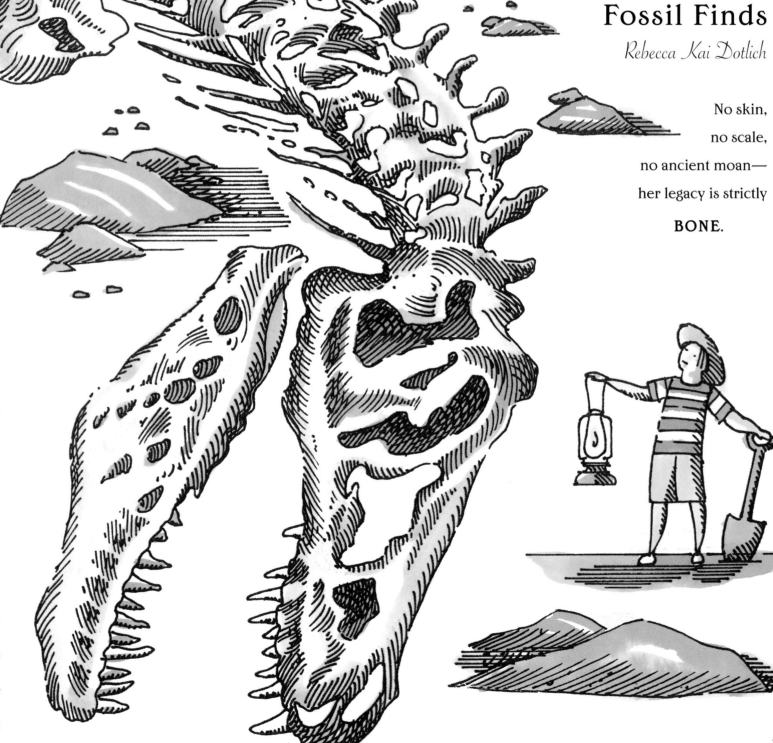

May 17, 2000:
Sue, a dinosaur, is exhibited in Chicago, Illinois

In South Dakota in 1990 Susan Hendrickson discovered bone fossils that later were assembled into the largest, most complete skeleton ever found of the *Tyrannosaurus rex*, a dinosaur that lived more than 67 million years ago.

In 1997, at an auction, the Field Museum in Chicago, Illinois, offered the highest price for the bones, more than $8 million.

After three years of laboriously putting Sue back together, she went on exhibit in the Field Museum.

Fossil Finds

Rebecca Kai Dotlich

No skin,
no scale,
no ancient moan—
her legacy is strictly
BONE.

May 30, 1868: Memorial Day first observed

The first observance of Memorial Day was held on May 30, 1868, to honor soldiers killed in the Civil War (1861–1865). Today Memorial Day is celebrated on the last Monday in May to honor all Americans who have given their lives during wartime. The event became a federal holiday in 1971.

Memorial Day

Constance Andrea Keremes

Daddy keeps the war in a shoebox
  tied up tight
        with a long white string.

On Memorial Day
  we open the box
        lift the lid
              and look inside.

Dog tags and pins and stars and stripes
all jumbled together like prizes in a gumball machine.

    Then Daddy puts my hand in his
    and tells me about the war

And I feel the meaning of Memorial Day

        in the warmth of Daddy's hands.

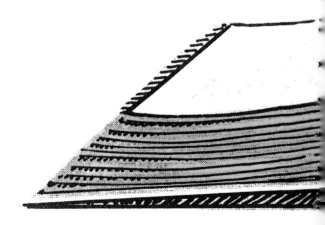

50

May 31: Birth date: Walter ("Walt") Whitman (1819–1892)

Whitman grew up in Brooklyn, New York. At the age of 12 he began to learn the printer's trade and fell in love with the written word. He worked as a teacher, printer, journalist, and, during the Civil War, a volunteer in military hospitals in Washington, D.C.

He published the first edition of *Leaves of Grass*, a volume of 12 untitled poems, when he was 36 years old. The work went through various editions throughout his entire life, ending with the "deathbed" edition containing more than 300 poems, published in 1892. *Leaves of Grass* is one of the world's most famous literary works.

Now Lift Me Close

Walt Whitman

Now lift me close to your face till I whisper,

What you are holding is in reality no book, nor part of a book;

It is a man, flush'd and full blooded—it is I—*So long*—

We must separate awhile—Here! take from my lips this kiss;

Whoever you are, I give it especially to you;

So long!—And I hope we shall meet again.

51

June

National Flag Week: The week including June 14

Father's Day: 3rd Sunday

Fink Day: 4th Friday, people named Fink from the world over gather for a reunion in Fink, TX

1	2	3	4
1792 Kentucky: 15th state to enter the Union **1796** Tennessee: 16th state to enter the Union	**1953** Queen Elizabeth II of England crowned	**1904** Birth date: Charles Drew, pioneer of preservation of blood for transfusion and blood banks	**1965** Astronaut Ed White II becomes the first American to walk in space

9	10	11	12
1790 *The Philadelphia Spelling Book* is the first book entered for U.S. copyright	**1922** Birth date: Judy Garland, singer, actress **1928** Birth date: Maurice Sendak, author, illustrator **1982** Birth date: Tara Lipinski, Olympic figure skater	*King Kamehameha I Day* Hawaiian holiday; only U.S. holiday honoring a king **1880** Birth date: Jeannette Rankin, first woman elected to the U.S. Congress	**1924** Birth date: George Herbert Walker Bush, 41st U.S. president **1929** Birth date: Anne Frank, author of *Anne Frank: The Diary of a Young Girl*

17	18	19	20
1882 Birth date: Igor Fëdorovich Stravinsky, Russian-born American composer **1925** First National Spelling Bee held	**1983** Sally Kristen Ride becomes the first American woman in space **1961** Birth date: Angela Johnson, author, poet	**1885** Packed into 214 crates, Statue of Liberty arrives in New York Harbor from France **1910** First Father's Day celebration	**1863** West Virginia: 35th state to enter the Union

25	26	27	28
1788 Virginia: 10th state to enter the Union	**1914?** Birth date: Mildred Ella ("Babe") Didrikson Zaharias, world-renowned athlete **1915** Birth date: Charlotte Zolotow, author, poet **1936** Birth date: Nancy Willard, author, poet	**1872** Birth date: Paul Laurence Dunbar, poet **1880** Birth date: Helen Adams Keller, author, lecturer **1922** First Newbery Medal awarded, to Hendrik van Loon for *The Story of Mankind* **1936** Birth date: Lucille Clifton, poet	**1902** Birth date: Richard Rodgers, composer

Helen Keller said:

"It is not possible for civilization to flow backwards while there is youth in the world."

June was named either for Juniores, the lower branch of the Roman Senate, or for Juno, the wife of Jupiter, a Roman god.

FLOWER: ROSE
BIRTHSTONE: PEARL
ZODIAC SIGN: CANCER, THE CRAB (JUNE 22–JULY 22)
CRABS ENJOY THE OUTDOORS BUT TAKE EQUAL PLEASURE IN HOME LIFE. FAMILY-ORIENTED, THEY LIKE BEING IN THEIR COMFORTABLE SHELLS.

5
496 B.C. Birth date: Socrates, Greek philosopher

6
1599 Birth date: Diego Rodríguez de Silva y Velázquez, Spanish artist

1954 Birth date: Cynthia Rylant, author, poet

7
1848 Birth date: Paul Gauguin, French artist

1917 Birth date: Gwendolyn Elizabeth Brooks, poet

1943 Birth date: Nikki Giovanni, poet

8
1867? Birth date: Frank Lloyd Wright, architect

13
1805 Lewis and Clark Expedition reaches the Great Falls of the Missouri River

14 *Flag Day*
1811 Birth date: Harriet Beecher Stowe, abolitionist, author of *Uncle Tom's Cabin*

1938 First Caldecott Medal awarded, to Dorothy Lathrop for *Animals of the Bible*

1948 Birth date: Laurence Yep, author

15
1836 Arkansas: 25th state to enter the Union

1924 U.S. Congress passes a law recognizing the citizenship of Native Americans

16
1963 Valentina Tereshkova, Russian cosmonaut, becomes the first woman in space

21 *First day of summer*
1788 New Hampshire: 9th state to enter the Union

1982 Birth date: Prince William, son of Prince Charles and Princess Diana of Great Britain

22
1949 Birth date: Mary Louise ("Meryl") Streep, actress, nominated for a record-setting thirteen Academy Awards

23
1868 Typewriter patented by Luther Sholes

1888 Frederick Douglass becomes the first African-American U.S. presidential candidate

1940 Birth date: Wilma Glodean Rudolph, track and field athlete

24
1916 Birth date: John Anthony Ciardi, poet

29
1577 Birth date: Peter Paul Rubens, Flemish artist

30
1917 Birth date: Lena Horne, actress, singer

WEATHER REPORT
On June 22, 1989, Rapid City, South Dakota, reported a record low of 39 degrees in contrast with a record high of 102 degrees three days earlier, June 19.

June 7: Birth date: Gwendolyn Elizabeth Brooks (1917–2000)

Brooks's first poem, "Eventide," was published when she was 13 years old. Between the ages of 16 and 17, she had close to 100 poems published in the *Chicago Defender*, the first African-American newspaper to have a national readership.

In 1950, she became the first African-American to win the Pulitzer Prize for Poetry.

Skipper

Gwendolyn Brooks

I looked in the fish-glass,
And what did I see.
A pale little gold fish
Looked sadly at me.
At the base of the bowl,
So still, he was lying.
"Are you dead, little fish?"
"Oh, no! But I'm dying."
I gave him fresh water
And the best of fish food—
But it was too late.
I did him no good.
I buried him by
Our old garden tree.
Our old garden tree
Will protect him for me.

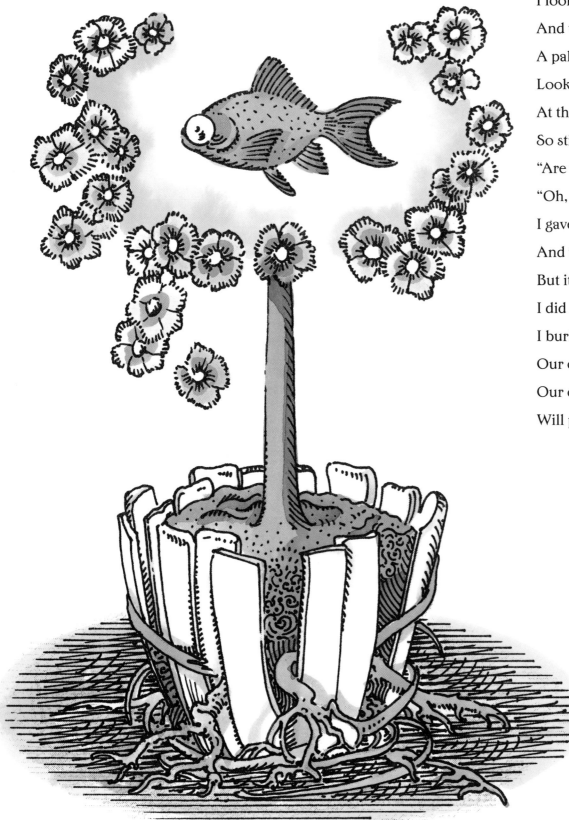

Father's Day came about through the efforts of Sonora Louise Smart Dodd of Spokane, Washington. After listening to a sermon on Mother's Day, she thought fathers should be honored too. Although the first Father's Day was held on June 19, 1910, in Spokane, it wasn't until 1972 that President Richard Milhous Nixon signed legislation designating the third Sunday in June for this holiday.

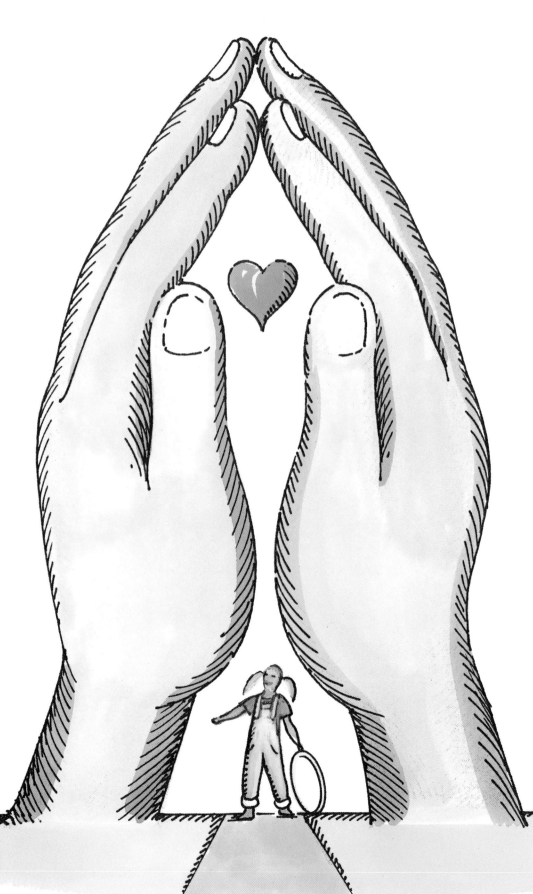

A Father's Hands

Rebecca Kai Dotlich

Gently shake

you awake.

Brush.

Braid.

Break eggs.

Write letters.

Patch tires.

Put out fires.

A father's hands

stack books.

Stir soup.

Pull weeds.

Lead.

Pound nails.

Steer sails.

A father's hands

lift.

Hold.

Build.   Fold.

Swing bats.

Feed cats.

Paint.   Sweep.

Peel.

Heal.

June 21:
First day of summer

From
Stay,
June,
Stay

Christina G. Rossetti

Stay, June, stay!—
If only we could stop the moon
And June!

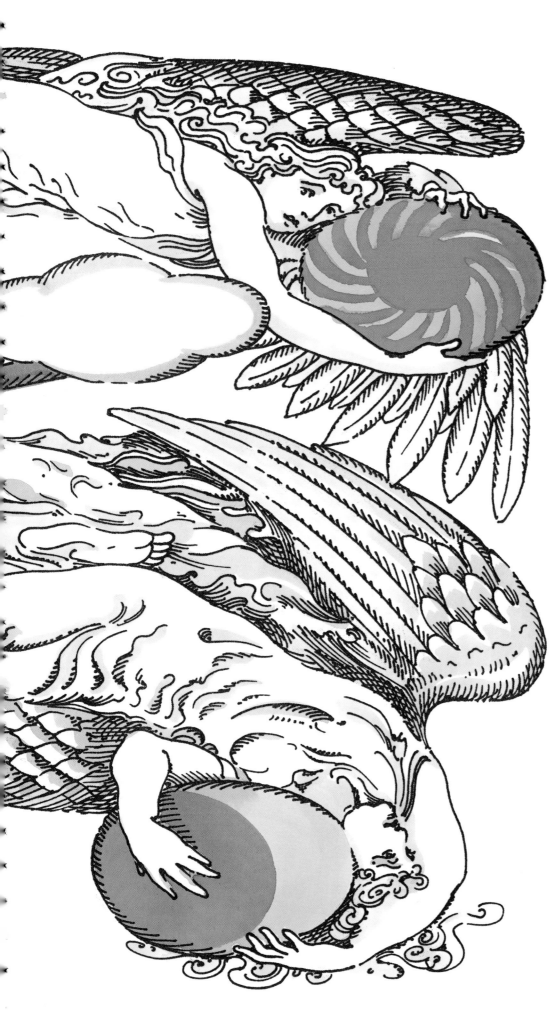

June 24: Birth date:
John Anthony Ciardi
(1916–1986)

Born in Boston, Massachusetts, Ciardi
wrote volumes of poems for children
and adults. "The River Is a Piece of
Sky" is from his first book of poems
for children, *The Reason for the Pelican*,
published in 1959.

In 1982, he received the National
Council of Teachers of English Award
for Excellence in Poetry for Children, an
award given for a poet's aggregate body
of work.

The River Is a Piece of Sky

John Ciardi

From the top of a bridge

The river below

Is a piece of sky—

> Until you throw
>
> A penny in
>
> Or a cockleshell
>
> Or a pebble or two
>
> Or a bicycle bell
>
> Or a cobblestone
>
> Or a fat man's cane—

And then you can see

It's a river again.

The difference you'll see

When you drop a penny:

The river has splashes,

The sky hasn't any.

June 26: Birth date: Mildred Ella ("Babe") Didrikson Zaharias (1914?–1956)

Nicknamed Babe after the legendary baseball player Babe Ruth, Zaharias, born in Port Arthur, Texas, was one of the greatest female athletes of all times. She excelled in a host of sports, including basketball, baseball, track, tennis, and golf. In 1932, she won two Olympic events—the javelin and the 80-meter hurdles. Six times she was voted "Woman of the Year" by the Associated Press.

First Lady of Twentieth-Century Sports

J. Patrick Lewis

Let me tell you a little story
    About Babe Zaharias.
She walked like you and she talked like me,
    But she wasn't like any of us.

She was born in outback Texas,
    Where the tallest tall tales grow,
And they stood in line to see her
    One-superwoman show.

Babe raced the wind and beat it,
    She high-hurdled the town,
She threw the javelin a mile—
    And caught it coming down.

Babe long-jumped over Texas,
    And put the shot so far,
It flew over Oklahoma
    Just like a shooting star.

And when she took up golfing,
    She had seventeen straight wins.
That's where the lady's story ends—
    And her legend then begins.

July

1 *Canada Day* **1961** Birth date: Carl Lewis, Olympic track star	**2** **1908** Birth date: Thurgood Marshall, first African-American to serve on the U.S. Supreme Court	**3** **1890** Idaho: 43rd state to enter the Union	**4** *Independence Day* **1872** Birth date: (John) Calvin Coolidge, 30th U.S. president **1900** Birth date: Louis ("Satchmo") Armstrong, jazz musician **1975** Fourth of July butterfly count, an annual event, begun by the Xerces Society
9 **1819** Birth date: Elias Howe, inventor of the sewing machine	**10** **1875** Birth date: Mary McLeod Bethune, educator **1890** Wyoming: 44th state to enter the Union **1928** Birth date: Patricia Hubbell, poet **1943** Birth date: Arthur Robert Ashe, Jr., tennis player **1951** Birth date: Rebecca Kai Dotlich, poet	**11** **1767** Birth date: John Quincy Adams, 6th U.S. president **1899** Birth date: Elwyn Brooks ("E. B.") White, author of *Charlotte's Web*	**12** **1817** Birth date: Henry David Thoreau, author of *Walden* **1884** Birth date: Amedeo Modigliani, Italian artist **1971** Birth date: Kristi Yamaguchi, Olympic figure skater
17 **1859** Birth date: Luis Muñoz Rivera, Puerto Rican patriot, poet **1932** Birth date: Karla Kuskin, poet	**18** **1921** Birth date: John Herschel Glenn, Jr., first American to orbit Earth **1976** Nadia Comaneci, age 14, becomes the first gymnast to receive a perfect score in the Olympic Games	**19** **1713** Birth date: John Newbery, first bookseller and publisher to specialize in children's books **1834** Birth date: Edgar Degas, French artist **1916** Birth date: Eve Merriam, poet	**20** **1969** Neil Armstrong is the first person to set foot on the moon
25 *Puerto Rico Constitution Day*	**26** **1788** New York: 11th state to enter the Union	**27** **1857** Birth date: José Celso Barbosa, Puerto Rican physician and patriot **1945** Birth date: Paul Bryan Janeczko, poet	**28** **1866** Birth date: Beatrix Potter, English artist, author of *The Tales of Peter Rabbit*

Henry David Thoreau said:

*"He who cannot read is worse than deaf and blind,
is yet but half alive, is still-born."*

July was named by Mark Antony in honor of Julius Caesar.

FLOWER: LARKSPUR
BIRTHSTONE: RUBY
ZODIAC SIGN: LEO, THE LION (JULY 23–AUGUST 22)
Like the lion, Leos are proud. They are risk takers who roar with self-confidence.

5
1810 Birth date: Phineas Taylor ("P. T.") Barnum, circus showman

6
1907 Birth date: Frida Kahlo, Mexican artist

1946 Birth date: George Walker Bush, 43rd U.S. president

7
1887 Birth date: Marc Chagall, Russian-born French artist

8
1776 First public reading of the Declaration of Independence, Philadelphia, PA

13
1923 Birth date: Ashley Bryan, author, poet, artist

14
1912 Birth date: Woodrow Wilson ("Woody") Guthrie, folk musician, writer of "This Land Is Your Land"

1913 Birth date: Gerald Rudolph Ford, 38th U.S. president

15 *St. Swithin's Day*
1606 Birth date: Rembrandt Harmenszoon van Rijn, Dutch artist

1779 Birth date: Clement Clarke Moore, author of *A Visit from St. Nicholas*

1906 Birth date: Richard Willard Armour, poet

16
1935 Birth date: Arnold Adoff, poet

21
1899 Birth date: Ernest Miller Hemingway, author, Nobel Prize winner

22
1849 Birth date: Emma Lazarus, poet

1898 Birth date: Stephen Vincent Benét, poet

1898 Birth date: Alexander Calder, sculptor

23
1827 First swimming school in the United States opened, Boston, MA. Pupils included John Quincy Adams and John James Audubon.

24
1783 Birth date: Simón Bolívar, South American revolutionary

1897 Birth date: Amelia Earhart, aviator, first woman to fly solo across the Atlantic

29
1958 National Aeronautics and Space Administration (NASA) established

30
1904 First international soccer match; Belgium and France compete

31
1965 Birth date: Joanne Kathleen ("J. K.") Rowling, English author of *Harry Potter* series

WEATHER REPORT

On July 4, 1956, a world record for the most rain falling in 1 minute
was set at Unionville, Maryland, a downpour of 1.23 inches.

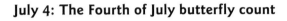

July 4: The Fourth of July butterfly count

Now sponsored by the North American Butterfly Association, each year on or near the Fourth of July thousands of volunteers throughout North America gather to identify and count butterflies.

In 2001, 474 butterfly counts were held in 48 states, Canada, and Mexico. More than 300,000 butterflies were counted. This event provides information to protect endangered butterfly species.

From
Sing-Song
Christina G. Rossetti

Brown and furry

Caterpillar in a hurry

Take your walk

To the shady leaf, or stalk,

Or what not.

Which may be the chosen spot.

No toad spy you,

Hovering bird of prey pass by you;

Spin and die,

To live again a butterfly.

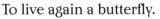

July 4, 1776: Independence Day

Representatives of the thirteen American colonies approved the Declaration of Independence on this date. Written by Thomas Jefferson, the document announced the colonies' separation from Great Britain to create the United States. The Declaration is one of the great political documents of history.

Fourth of July Parade *Anonymous*

Hear the blare of bugles,
Hear the beat of drums,
Hear the sound of marching feet.
Down the street there comes,
 Playing, marching,
 Marching, playing,
 In the sun and shade,
 All the music,
 All the color
 Of the Fourth's parade.

See the buglers blowing,
See the drummers pound,
See the feet go up and down
To the music's sound.
 Playing, marching,
 Marching, playing,
 In the shade and sun,
 All the color,
 All the music,
 Says the Fourth's begun.

July 5: Birth date:
Phineas Taylor Barnum (1810–1891)

Barnum opened his famous circus, the Greatest Show on Earth, in 1871. Eventually he merged with the Ringling Brothers to create Ringling Brothers and Barnum & Bailey Circus, a troupe that continues to tour throughout America.

At the heart of the circus is . . .

The Ringmaster

Lee Bennett Hopkins

The ringmaster shouts and gaily sings
About so many circus things.

"In ring one," he proudly calls,
"Are silky-black seals
Bouncing fire-red balls.

And look in ring three
For you now will see
Gertrude, the chimpanzee, ice-skate and ski.

In the center ring there's a peculiar gent
Who will float on balloons
To the top of our tent."

The ringmaster stands so very tall, shouting:

"It's Circus-Time
For one. For all!"

July 15: St. Swithin's Day

When Swithin, bishop of Winchester, England, died in 862, he was buried outside Winchester Cathedral at his request. After he was made a saint, his body was moved inside the cathedral on July 15, 931, a day of teeming rain. The downpour continued for the next 40 days, leading people to believe St. Swithin preferred to remain out in the open.

According to legend, if it rains on July 15, it will rain for 40 days. An old English saying goes:

St. Swithin's Day, if thou dost rain,

for forty days it will remain;

St. Swithin's Day, if thou be fair,

for forty days 'twill rain nae mair.

July 22: Birth date: Emma Lazarus (1849–1887)

Lazarus is best known for her sonnet "The New Colossus." In 1903 the poem was engraved on the pedestal of the Statue of Liberty. The verse has become a welcome to the United States for thousands of immigrants.

The New Colossus

Emma Lazarus

Not like the brazen giant of Greek fame,
With conquering limbs astride from land to land;
Here at our sea-washed, sunset gates shall stand
A mighty woman with a torch, whose flame
Is the imprisoned lightning, and her name
Mother of Exiles. From her beacon-hand
Glows world-wide welcome; her mild eyes command
The air-bridged harbor that twin cities frame.
"Keep, ancient lands, your storied pomp!" cries she
With silent lips. "Give me your tired, your poor,
Your huddled masses yearning to breathe free,
The wretched refuse of your teeming shore.
Send these, the homeless, tempest-tost to me,
I lift my lamp beside the golden door!"

August

1
1779 Birth date: Francis Scott Key, writer of "The Star-Spangled Banner"

1818 Birth date: Maria Mitchell, first woman professional astronomer

1819 Birth date: Herman Melville, author of *Moby Dick*

1876 Colorado: 38th state to enter the Union

2
1754 Birth date: Pierre Charles L'Enfant, French architect who created the plans for Washington, D.C.

1858 First U.S. mailboxes installed, Boston, MA, and New York, NY

3
1492 Christopher Columbus set sail from Palos, Spain, with his three ships, *Nina*, *Pinta*, and *Santa María*

4
1792 Birth date: Percy Bysshe Shelley, English poet

9
1819 Birth date: William Thomas Green Monton, first dentist to use ether as a general anesthetic

1906 Birth date: Pamela Lyndon ("P. L.") Travers, Australian author of *Mary Poppins* series

10
1821 Missouri: 24th state to enter the Union

1874 Birth date: Herbert Clark Hoover, 31st U.S. president

11
1944 Birth date: Joanna Cole, author of *The Magic School Bus* series

12
1859 Birth date: Katharine Lee Bates, lyricist of "America, the Beautiful"

1930 Birth date: Mary Ann Hoberman, poet

17
1786 Birth date: David ("Davy") Crockett, frontiersman

1926 Birth date: Myra Cohn Livingston, poet

18
1587 Birth date: Virginia Dare, first child of English parents to be born in America

1934 Birth date: Roberto Clemente, Puerto Rican baseball player

19
1871 Birth date: Orville Wright, aviation pioneer

1902 Birth date: Ogden Nash, poet

1946 Birth date: William Jefferson ("Bill") Clinton, 42nd U.S. president

20
1833 Birth date: Benjamin Harrison, 23rd U.S. president

25
1918 Birth date: Leonard Bernstein, composer

1927 Birth date: Althea Gibson, tennis champion

1939 Film *The Wizard of Oz* released

26
1920 Passage of the 19th Amendment, giving women the right to vote

27
1908 Birth date: Lyndon Baines Johnson, 36th U.S. president

28
1958 Birth date: Scott Hamilton, Olympic figure skater

1963 March on Washington, D.C.; Martin Luther King, Jr., delivers his famed "I Have a Dream" speech

Lyndon Baines Johnson said:

"Tomorrow is ours to win or to lose."

Julius Caesar's adopted nephew and heir, Gaius Julius Caesar Octavianus, was the first Roman emperor to receive the title Augustus, meaning "reverend." Augustus named the month for himself.

FLOWER: POPPY
BIRTHSTONE: SARDONYX
ZODIAC SIGN: VIRGO, THE VIRGIN (AUGUST 23–SEPTEMBER 22)
VIRGOS ARE GREAT THINKERS. HIGHLY ORGANIZED, THEY HAVE A UNIQUE ABILITY TO SOLVE PROBLEMS.

5
1930 Birth date: Neil Alden Armstrong, astronaut

1989 Largest game of musical chairs—8,238 players—played in Singapore

6
1809 Birth date: Alfred, Lord Tennyson, English poet

1926 Gertrude Ederle becomes the first woman to swim the English Channel

7
1904 Birth date: Ralph Johnson Bunche, United Nations diplomat, first African-American to win Nobel Prize for Peace

8
1866 Birth date: Matthew Alexander Henson, polar explorer

1884 Birth date: Sara Teasdale, poet

13
1860 Birth date: Phoebe Anne ("Annie Oakley") Moses, sharpshooter

14
1863 Birth date: Ernest Lawrence Thayer, author of "Casey at the Bat"

15
1771 Birth date: Sir Walter Scott, Scottish author of *Ivanhoe*

16
1862 Birth date: Amos Alonzo Stagg, football player, who became the game's greatest innovator

21
1929 Birth date: X. J. Kennedy, poet

1959 Hawaii: 50th state to enter the Union

22
1862 Birth date: Claude Achille Debussy, French composer

23
1869 Birth date: Edgar Lee Masters, poet

1912 Birth date: Gene Kelly, dancer, actor

24
1869 Waffle iron patented by Cornelius Swartout

1890 Birth date: Duke Kahanamoku, best swimmer in the world, 1912–1928

29
1809 Birth date: Oliver Wendell Holmes, poet, author

1920 Birth date: Charlie ("Bird") Parker, jazz musician

30
1797 Birth date: Mary Godwin Wollstonecraft Shelley, English author of *Frankenstein*

1983 Guion Stewart Bluford, Jr., becomes the first African-American astronaut

31
1897 Motion-picture camera patented by Thomas Alva Edison

WEATHER REPORT

On August 4, 1980, a record 42 days of 100-degree heat came to an end in Texas.

Though he drowned at the age of 29, Shelley is considered one of the greatest poets of the English language. Shelley, who lived in Italy, paid tribute to Pisa, Italy, in . . .

Evening: Ponte al Mare, Pisa

Percy Bysshe Shelley

The sun is set; the swallows are asleep;

    The bats are flitting fast in the grey air;

The slow soft toads out of damp corners creep,

    And evening's breath, wandering here and there

Over the quivering surface of the stream,

Wakes not one ripple from its summer dream.

There is no dew on the dry grass to-night,

    Nor damp within the shadow of the trees;

The wind is intermitting, dry, and light;

    And in the inconstant motion of the breeze

The dust and straws are driven up and down,

And whirled about the pavement of the town.

Within the surface of the fleeting river

    The wrinkled image of the city lay,

Immovably unquiet, and for ever

    It trembles, but it never fades away . . .

Tennyson, one of England's most important poets, was born in Somersby, Lincolnshire. He began publishing poetry at the age of 18. In 1850, he was named poet laureate of Britain.

The Eagle *Alfred, Lord Tennyson*

He clasps the crag with crooked hands;

Close to the sun in lonely lands,

Ring'd with the azure world, he stands.

The wrinkled sea beneath him crawls;

He watches from his mountain walls,

And like a thunderbolt he falls.

August 14: Birth date: Ernest Lawrence Thayer (1863–1940)

Born in Lawrence, Massachusetts, Thayer attended and was graduated magna cum laude from Harvard University. He was a frequent contributor to the *San Francisco Examiner*, and "Casey at the Bat" appeared in the newspaper on June 3, 1888. Since then the verse has become a well-known classic throughout the world.

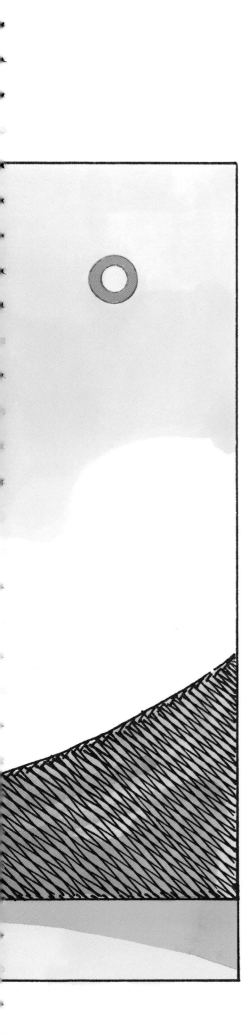

Casey at the Bat

Ernest Lawrence Thayer

The outlook wasn't brilliant for the Mudville nine that day;
The score stood four to two with but one inning more to play.
And then, when Cooney died at first, and Barrows did the same,
A sickly silence fell upon the patrons of the game.

A straggling few got up to go in deep despair. The rest
Clung to that hope which springs eternal in the human breast;
They thought, If only Casey could but get a whack at that
We'd put up even money now, with Casey at the bat.

But Flynn preceded Casey, as did also Jimmy Blake,
And the former was a lulu and the latter was a cake;
So upon that stricken multitude grim melancholy sat,
For there seemed but little chance of Casey's getting to the bat.

But Flynn let drive a single, to the wonderment of all,
And Blake, the much despised, tore the cover off the ball;
And when the dust had lifted, and men saw what had occurred,
There was Jimmy safe at second, and Flynn a-hugging third.

Then from 5,000 throats and more there rose a lusty yell;
It rumbled through the valley, it rattled in the dell;
It knocked upon the mountain and recoiled upon the flat,
For Casey, mighty Casey, was advancing to the bat.

There was ease in Casey's manner as he stepped into his place;
There was pride in Casey's bearing and a smile on Casey's face.
And when, responding to the cheers, he lightly doffed his hat,
No stranger in the crowd could doubt 'twas Casey at the bat.

Ten thousand eyes were on him as he rubbed his hands with dirt,
Five thousand tongues applauded when he wiped them on his shirt;
Then while the writhing pitcher ground the ball into his hip,
Defiance gleamed from Casey's eye, a sneer curled Casey's lip.

And now the leather-covered sphere came hurtling through the air,
And Casey stood a-watching it in haughty grandeur there.
Close by the sturdy batsman the ball unheeded sped—
"That ain't my style," said Casey. "Strike one," the umpire said.

From the benches, black with people, there went up a muffled roar,
Like the beating of the storm waves on a stern and distant shore.
"Kill him! Kill the umpire!" shouted someone on the stand.
And it's likely they'd have killed him had not Casey raised his hand.

With a smile of Christian charity great Casey's visage shone;
He stilled the rising tumult, he bade the game go on;
He signaled to the pitcher, and once more the spheroid flew;
But Casey still ignored it, and the umpire said, "Strike two."

"Fraud!" cried the maddened thousands, and echo answered fraud;
But one scornful look from Casey and the audience was awed;
They saw his face grown stern and cold, they saw his muscles strain,
And they knew that Casey wouldn't let that ball go by again.

The sneer is gone from Casey's lip, his teeth are clenched in hate,
He pounds with cruel violence his bat upon the plate;
And now the pitcher holds the ball, and now he lets it go,
And now the air is shattered by the force of Casey's blow.

Oh, somewhere in the favored land the sun is shining bright,
The band is playing somewhere, and somewhere hearts are light;
And somewhere men are laughing, and somewhere children shout,
But there is no joy in Mudville—mighty Casey has struck out.

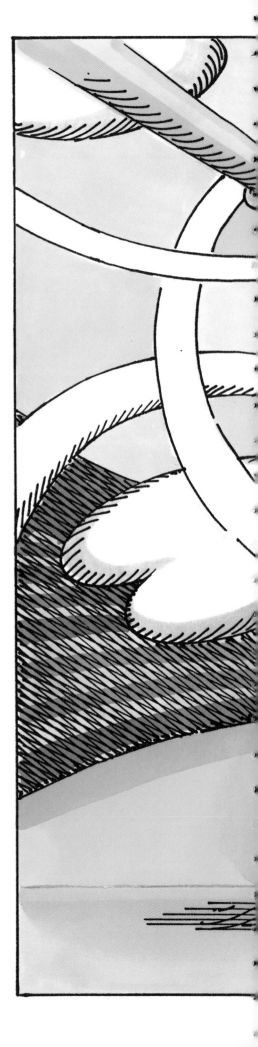

After publishing poetry and nonfiction works for adults, Kennedy turned his pen to write for children in 1975. He is a modern master of light verse and his witty words have earned him many awards and honors.

There are many of us who are. . .

Wishing for
Winter in Summer

X. J. Kennedy

Why won't it snow in summer?
I wish there was a wizard
Who'd wave his wand and say the word
And sock us with a blizzard.

I've swum so much I'm half dissolved.
I'm tired of riding bicycles.
I want to throw a snowball and
Knock down some rooftop icicles.

You can't make snowmen out of grass—
That just won't get you far.
I want to see my dad put chains
And snow tires on the car.

I want to hear the firehouse horn
Go *Bawp! No school today,*
Roll over, and go back to sleep
And dream of summer play.

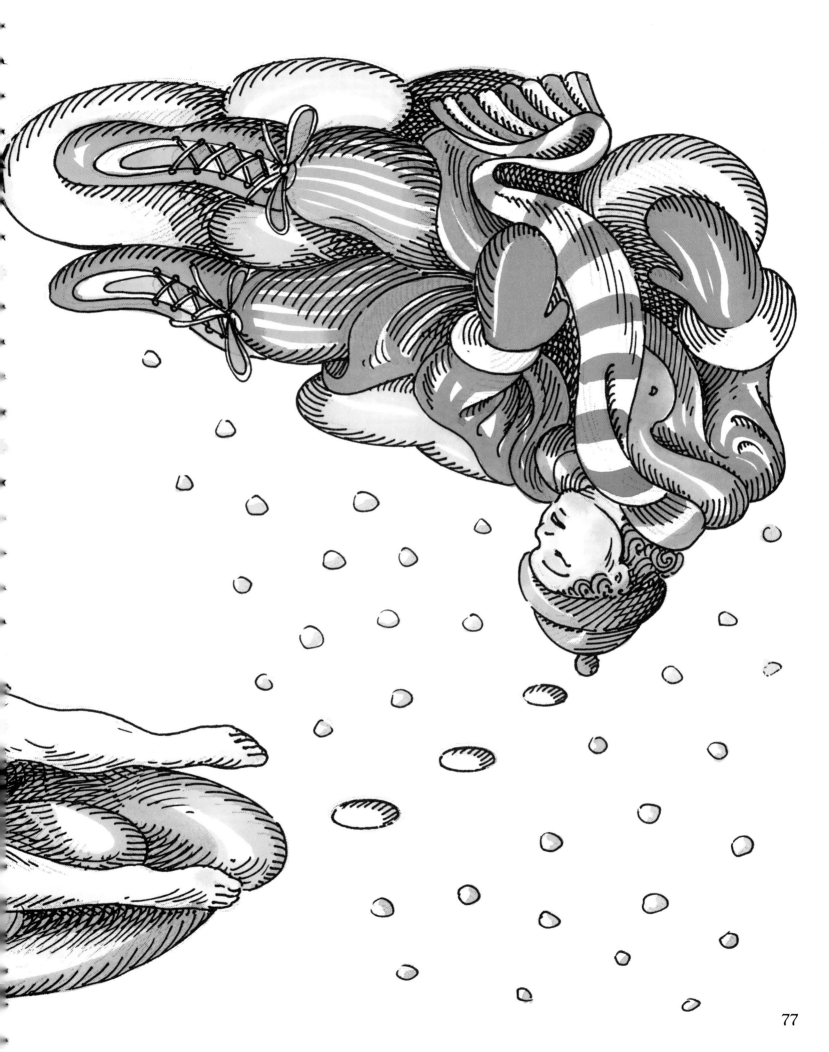

September

Library Card Sign-Up Month

Labor Day: 1st Monday

National Hispanic Heritage Month: September 15–October 15

Rosh Hashanah (Jewish New Year): September/October: begins on the 1st day of Tishri according to the Hebrew calendar

Yom Kippur (Day of Atonement): September/October: begins on the 10th day of Tishri according to the Hebrew calendar

1 **1875** Birth date: Edgar Rice Burroughs, author of *Tarzan*	**2** **1838** Birth date: Queen Liliuokalani, Hawaii's last monarch	**3** **1976** Landing on Mars of U.S. space probes Viking I and Viking II	**4** **1968** Birth date: Mike Piazza, baseball player
9 **1850** California: 31st state to enter the Union **1906** Birth date: Aileen Fisher, poet	**10** **1846** Sewing machine patented by Elias Howe	**11** **1862** Birth date: William Sydney Porter ("O. Henry"), author of "The Gift of the Magi"	**12** **1913** Birth date: Jesse Owens, Olympic track and field champion
17 **1787** Constitution Day, U.S. Constitution officially signed **1883** Birth date: William Carlos Williams, physician, poet	**18** **1851** First issue of *New York Times* newspaper published; 4 pages for a penny	**19** **1867** Birth date: Arthur Rackham, English illustrator	**20** **1885** Birth date: Ferdinand Joseph La Menthe ("Jelly Roll") Morton, musician, jazz innovator **1928** Birth date: Donald Hall, poet
25 **1932** Birth date: Shelby ("Shel") Silverstein, poet, composer **1981** Sandra Day O'Connor becomes the first woman to serve on the U.S. Supreme Court	**26** **1774** Birth date: John Chapman ("Johnny Appleseed"), legendary apple-tree planter **1888** Birth date: Thomas Stearns ("T. S.") Eliot, poet	**27** **1822** Birth date: Hiram Rhodes Revels, first African-American senator	**28** **1909** Birth date: Alfred G. ("Al") Capp, cartoonist, creator of *L'il Abner* **1924** Birth date: James Berry, Jamaican-born British poet

T. S. Eliot said:

"There is not enough silence."

From the Latin word septem *meaning "seven," September was the seventh month in the Roman calendar until* 45 B.C., *when Julius Caesar revised the calendar.*

FLOWER: ASTER
BIRTHSTONE: SAPPHIRE
ZODIAC SIGN: LIBRA, THE SCALES (SEPTEMBER 23–OCTOBER 22)
LIBRANS ARE STRONG, DETERMINED LEADERS YET AFFECTIONATE AND SYMPATHETIC TO ALL.

5
1952 Birth date: Paul Fleischman, author, poet

6
1860 Birth date: Jane Addams, social reformer, Nobel Peace Prize winner

7
1860 Birth date: Anna Mary Robertson ("Grandma") Moses, artist

1917 Birth date: Jacob Lawrence, artist

8
1892 First appearance in print of the Pledge of Allegiance, in *Youth's Companion*

1940 Birth date: Jack Prelutsky, poet

13
1916 Birth date: Roald Dahl, English author

14
1716 Lighting of first lighthouse built in the United States, Little Brewster Island in Boston Harbor, MA

15
1857 Birth date: William Howard Taft, 27th U.S. president

16
1898 Birth date: Hans Augusto ("H. A.") Rey, creator of *Curious George*

21 *First day of autumn*
1789 U.S. Post Office established

22
1929 Birth date: Ann Grifalconi, artist, author

1985 A jigsaw puzzle 814 feet long, 54 feet wide, containing 15,520 pieces built in Keene, NH

23
1838 Birth date: Victoria Claflin Woodhull, first woman to run for U.S. presidency

1846 Planet Neptune discovered by German astronomer Johanne Galle

24
1898 Birth date: Harry Behn, poet

1936 Birth date: Jim Henson, creator of *The Muppets*

29
1901 Birth date: Enrico Fermi, Nobel Prize–winning physicist

30
1841 Stapler patented by Samuel Slocum

1962 Birth date: Janet Siu Wong, poet, author

WEATHER REPORT
Hailstones weighing up to 1.67 pounds fell in Coffeyville, Kansas, on September 3, 1970, setting a world record.

Labor Day: 1st Monday

Matthew Maguire, a machinist from Paterson, New Jersey, and Peter J. McGuire, a carpenter from New York, New York, are credited with suggesting a day to honor working people. They started the first Labor Day parade in New York City in 1882.

In 1887, Oregon became the first state to make Labor Day a legal holiday. President Grover Cleveland signed a bill in 1894, proclaiming Labor Day a national holiday.

Labor Day *Marci Ridlon*

First Monday in September

that's when we remember

to honor workers who toil long.

Their efforts make our country strong.

We give a gift they all like best;

We give them all a day of rest!

From
James Lee *Robert Browning*

Ah, love, but a day,

    And the world has changed!

The sun's away,

    And the bird's estranged;

The wind has dropped,

    And the sky's deranged:

Summer has stopped.

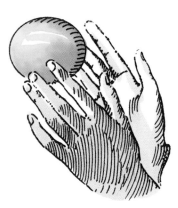

September 26: Birth date:
John Chapman ("Johnny Appleseed") (1774–1845)

Raggedly dressed, Chapman wandered for forty years through
Ohio, Indiana, and Pennsylvania, sowing apple seeds and
traveling hundreds of miles to tend his orchards.
Attributed to him is . . .

Oh, the Lord is good to me,

And so I thank the Lord,

For giving me the things I need:

The sun, the rain and the apple seed:

The Lord is good to me.

81

September 26: Birth date: Thomas Stearns ("T. S.") Eliot (1888–1965)

American-born British poet Eliot received the 1948 Nobel Prize in Literature. His book *Old Possum's Book of Practical Cats* was the basis of *Cats*, a record-breaking worldwide stage hit.

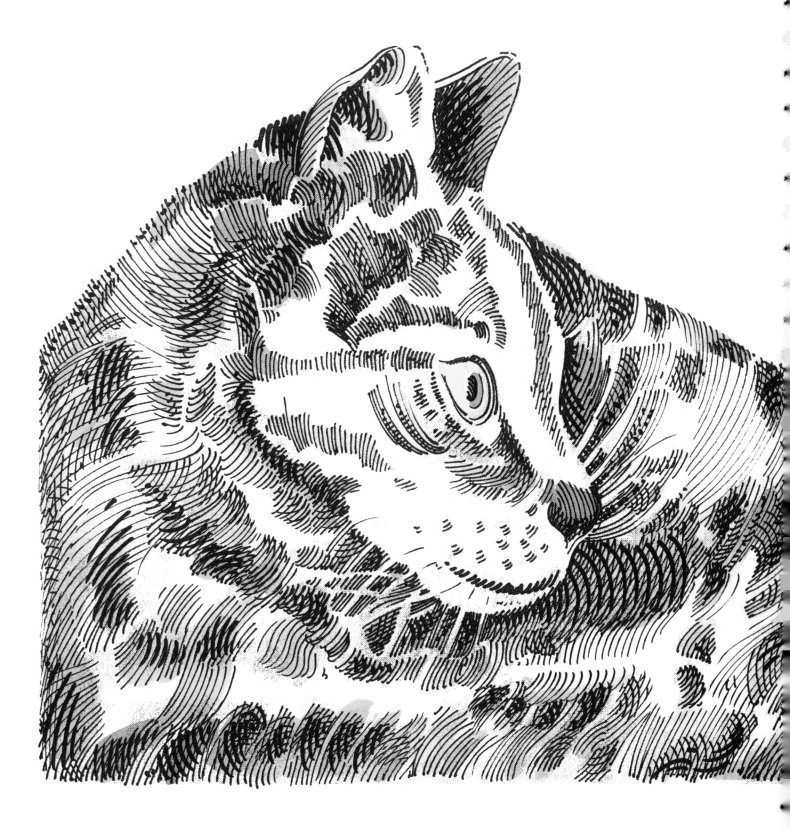

The Naming of Cats

T. S. Eliot

The Naming of Cats is a difficult matter,

    It isn't just one of your holiday games;

You may think at first I'm as mad as a hatter

When I tell you, a cat must have THREE DIFFERENT NAMES.

First of all, there's the name that the family use daily,

    Such as Peter, Augustus, Alonzo or James,

Such as Victor or Jonathan, George or Bill Bailey—

    All of them sensible everyday names.

There are fancier names if you think they sound sweeter,

    Some for the gentlemen, some for the dames:

Such as Plato, Admetus, Electra, Demeter—

    But all of them sensible everyday names.

But I tell you, a cat needs a name that's particular,

    A name that's peculiar, and more dignified,

Else how can he keep up his tail perpendicular,

    Or spread out his whiskers, or cherish his pride?

Of names of this kind, I can give you a quorum,

    Such as Munkustrap, Quaxo, or Coricopat,

Such as Bombalurina, or else Jellylorum—

    Names that never belong to more than one cat.

But above and beyond there's still one name left over,

    And that is the name that you never will guess;

The name that no human research can discover—

    But THE CAT HIMSELF KNOWS, and will never confess.

When you notice a cat in profound meditation,

    The reason, I tell you, is always the same:

His mind is engaged in a rapt contemplation

    Of the thought, of the thought, of the thought of his name:

        His ineffable effable

        Effanineffable

Deep and inscrutable singular Name.

In 1968, President Lyndon Baines Johnson set aside a week to honor Hispanic Americans. In 1988, the celebration was extended when President Ronald Reagan designated September 15 to October 15 National Hispanic Heritage Month.

Today more than 37 million Hispanics live in the United States.

Me x 2   Yo x 2

Jane Medina

I read times two.	Leo por dos.
I write times two.	Escribo por dos
I think, I dream,	Pienso y sueño
I cry times two.	Y lloro por dos.
I laugh times two.	Yo río por dos
I'm right times two.	Grito por dos
I sing, I ask	Canto, pregunto
I try times two.	Intento por dos.
I do twice as much	Hago mucho más
As most people do,	Que hacen todos ellos,
'Cause most speak one,	Porque yo hablo dos:
But I speak two!	Lo doble que aquéllos.

October

Columbus Day: 2nd Monday

1 **1924** Birth date: James Earl ("Jimmy") Carter, Jr., 39th U.S. president	**2** **1869** Birth date: Mahatma Mohandas Karamchand Gandhi, Indian political and spiritual leader **1967** Thurgood Marshall becomes the first African-American to serve on the U.S. Supreme Court	**3** **1916** Birth date: James Herriot, Scottish veterinarian, author of *All Creatures Great and Small*	**4** **1822** Birth date: Rutherford Birchard Hayes, 19th U.S. president **1957** *Sputnik I* is launched by the Soviet Union, marking beginning of the space age
9 *Han-gul Day* Celebration of King Sejong's proclamation of the official Korean alphabet in 1446, invented in 1443 **1855** Calliope, a steam organ with an 8-hole keyboard, patented by John Stoddard	**10** **1813** Birth date: Giuseppe Verdi, Italian composer	**11** **1884** Birth date: (Anna) Eleanor Roosevelt, "First Lady of the World"	**12** **1492** Columbus Day (traditional), landing of Christopher Columbus in the New World, possibly in the Bahamas
17 **1711** Birth date: Jupiter Hammon, first African-American published poet **1956** Birth date: Mae Jemison, first woman African-American astronaut	**18** **1921** Pop-up toaster patented by Charles Strite **1961** Birth date: Wynton Marsalis, jazz musician	**19** **1850** Birth date: Annie Smith Peck, world-renowned mountain climber	**20** **1859** Birth date: John Dewey, educator **1950** Birth date: Nikki Grimes, poet, author
25 **1340?** Birth date: Geoffrey Chaucer, English poet, author of *The Canterbury Tales* **1881** Birth date: Pablo Ruiz Picasso, Spanish artist	**26** **1825** Erie Canal opens	**27** **1858** Birth date: Theodore Roosevelt, 26th U.S. president **1904** New York City subway begins operation	**28** **1914** Birth date: Jonas Edward Salk, physician, developed polio vaccine

President Jimmy Carter said:

"Wherever life takes us there are always moments of wonder."

From the Latin word octo, *meaning "eight," October was the 8th month of the Roman calendar.*

FLOWER: MARIGOLD
BIRTHSTONE: OPAL
ZODIAC SIGN: SCORPIO, THE SCORPION (OCTOBER 23—NOVEMBER 21)
SCORPIOS ARE HONEST, HELPFUL, AND THE MOST LOYAL OF FRIENDS.

5
1829 Birth date: Chester Alan Arthur, 21st U.S. president

6
1897 Birth date: Florence Siebert, physician, developed test for tuberculosis

1973 Birth date: Rebecca Lobo, basketball player

7
1955 Birth date: Yo-Yo Ma, cellist

8
1943 Birth date: Robert Lawrence ("R. L.") Stine, author

13
1754 Birth date: Mary Ludwig Hays McCauley ("Molly Pitcher"), Revolutionary War heroine

14
1644 Birth date: William Penn, founder of Pennsylvania

1890 Birth date: Dwight David Eisenhower, 34th U.S. president

1894 Birth date: Edward Estlin ("E. E.") Cummings, poet

15
1951 Premiere of television's first smash hit, *I Love Lucy*; it ran 10 years

16
1758 Birth date: Noah Webster, publisher of *An American Dictionary of the English Language*

1942 Birth date: Joseph Bruchac, author, poet

21
1833 Birth date: Alfred Bernhard Nobel, Swedish inventor of dynamite who established the Nobel Prizes

1917 Birth date: John Berks ("Dizzy") Gillespie, jazz musician

22
1811 Birth date: Franz Liszt, Hungarian composer

23
1906 Birth date: Gertrude Caroline Ederle, Olympic champion, first woman to swim the English Channel

1940 Birth date: Edson Arantes do Nascimento ("Pelé"), soccer great

24 *United Nations Day*
Commemorates founding in 1945

1788 Birth date: Sarah Josepha Buell Hale, author of "Mary Had a Little Lamb," first woman editor in the United States

1919 Birth date: Felice Holman, author, poet

29
1933 Birth date: Valerie Worth, poet

1969 Internet created

30
1735 Birth date: John Adams, 2nd U.S. president

31 *Halloween*
1860 Birth date: Juliette Magill Kinzie Gordon Low, founder of Girl Scouts

1864 Nevada: 36th state to enter the Union

1941 Mount Rushmore National Monument, near Keystone, SD, completed after 14 years

WEATHER REPORT

On October 3, 1912, the longest dry spell of record in the United States began as Bagdad, California, went 767 days without a drop of rain.

Born in West Hartford, Connecticut, Webster was an educator and journalist. In the 1780s he compiled an elementary spelling book that eventually sold millions of copies. The book helped standardize spelling and pronunciation in the United States.

His fascination with words led to the compilation of *An American Dictionary of the English Language* published on April 14, 1828, a massive project consisting of two volumes with 70,000 entries—from *a* to *zygomatic*.

Treasure Words

Rebecca Kai Dotlich

Words are magic—
quiet, loud.
Steady, strong,
slow, proud.
Whisper, shout—
let them out—
hold words close,
toss afar,
see them sparkle—
each a star.
Thread words on
a silver chain,
let words touch you
warm as rain.
Written, read, said, heard—
delight in, sip on,
treasure words.

October 16: Birth date: Joseph Bruchac (1942–)

Bruchac, of Abenaki Indian and Slovak descent, is one of America's most respected and widely published Native American authors. In addition to poetry, he has written novels and biographies and has retold numerous Native American legends. He lives in the foothills of the Adirondack Mountains in New York, in the same house in which he grew up.

In the Moon of Falling Leaves
Joseph Bruchac

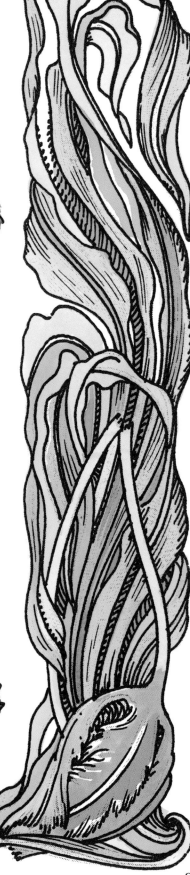

I was born in the Moon of Falling Leaves,
that time when summer's harvest
falls from every maple tree,
painting the forest trails
golden as sunlight
and crimson as Great Bear's blood.

Each October brings back the scent
of fires burning on the hills,
the first etchings of frost
on my bedroom windows,
the departing wings
of a thousand geese
cutting the clear cold sky.

There is no time closer to my heart,
than this season of changes
when the balance tips between
darkness and light,
when the last flowers
nod in our garden,
when so many things
are about to end,
so many about to begin.

October 23:
Birth date: Edson
Arantes do Nascimento
("Pelé") (1940–)

Pelé and soccer are synonymous.
Born in Três Corações, Brazil, Pelé is the most
recognized athlete in world sports. In soccer he holds
every major record in Brazil, scoring 1,281 goals in
1,363 games, the only player to score 1,000 goals in
a career.
Soccer, the most popular international sport,
has been an Olympic game since 1900.

Soccer

Lee Bennett Hopkins

Twenty-two

prayers

on

reverent grass

kick

dribble

trap

pass—

sprint

run

tackle

fall—

all

for the

love

of a

sacred

ball.

October 27, 1904: Opening of the New York City subway system

One of the world's busiest systems of transportation, the New York City subway serves more than 3.8 million people each day (4.5 million on weekdays).

Subways Are People

Lee Bennett Hopkins

Subways are people—

    People standing

    People sitting

    People swaying to and fro

    Some in suits

    Some in tatters

    People I will never know.

    Some with glasses

    Some without

    Boy with smile

    Girl with frown

    People dashing

    Steel flashing

    Up and down and 'round the town.

Subways are people—

    People old

    People new

    People always on the go

    Racing, running, rushing people

    People I will never know.

October 31: Halloween

Halloween comes from the ancient Celtic harvest festival Samhain, a time when people believed spirits of the dead roamed the earth.

Halloween became popular in the United States in the early 1800s, when immigrants from Ireland and Scotland introduced such activities as bobbing for apples and lighting jack-o'-lanterns.

E. E. Cummings, born on October 14, 1894, wrote a "devilish" poem that is a perfect ode to this magical night.

From
Chansons Innocentes, II

E. E. Cummings

hist   whist

little ghostthings

tip-toe

twinkle-toe

whisk   look out for the old woman

with the wart on her nose

what she'll do to yer

nobody knows

little twitchy

witches and tingling

goblins

hob-a-nob   hob-a-nob

for she knows the devil   ooch

the devil   ouch

the devil

ach   the great

little hoppy happy

toad in tweeds

tweeds

little itchy mousies

green

dancing

devil

with scuttling

eyes   rustle and run   and

hidehidehide

whisk

devil

devil

devil

wheeEEE

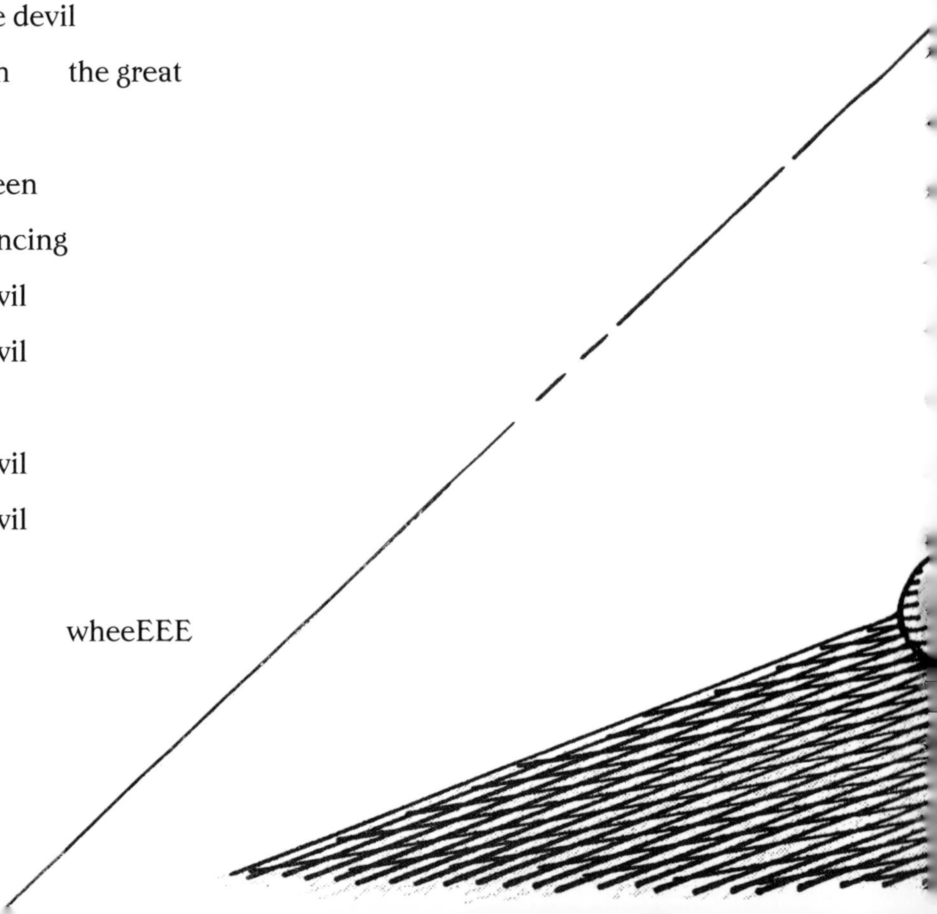

 November

Native American Heritage Month
Election Day: 1st Tuesday after the 1st Monday
National Children's Book Week: Week before Thanksgiving
Thanksgiving: Last Thursday
Hanukkah: November–December: 8-day Festival of Lights beginning on the 25th day of Kislev, according to the Hebrew calendar
Ramadan: November–December: Islamic holy month of fasting, 9th month of the Islamic calendar

1 *Día de los Muertos,* or *Day of the Dead*
Mexican holiday honoring ancestors

1848 First medical school for women opened, Boston, MA

1959 Hockey mask invented by Jacques Plante, hockey player of Canada

2
1734 Birth date: Daniel Boone, frontiersman

1795 Birth date: James Knox Polk, 11th U.S. president

1865 Birth date: Warren Gamaliel Harding, 29th U.S. president

1889 North Dakota: 39th state to enter the Union

1889 South Dakota: 40th state to enter the Union

3
1903 Birth date: Walker Evans, photographer

1957 Laika, a dog, becomes the first animal in space, aboard the Soviet spaceship *Sputnik 2*

4
1922 King Tutankhamen's tomb discovered in Egypt, one of the most important archaeological discoveries of modern times

9
1934 Birth date: Carl Sagan, astronomer

10
1903 Windshield wiper patented by Mary Anderson

11 *Veterans Day*
1851 Telescope patented by Alvan Clark

1889 Washington: 42nd state to enter the Union

12
1815 Birth date: Elizabeth Cady Stanton, suffragist

1840 Birth date: François Auguste René Rodin, French sculptor

17
1869 Suez Canal opens

18
1789 Birth date: Jacques Mandé Daguerre, French inventor of the daguerreotype, first practical method of photography

1923 Birth date: Alan Bartlett Shepard, Jr., astronaut, first American in space

1928 Mickey Mouse's first appearance, in the Walt Disney animated film *Steamboat Willie*

19 *Puerto Rico Discovery Day*
1831 Birth date: James Abram Garfield, 20th U.S. president

20
1858 Birth date: Selma Ottiliana Lovisa Lagerlöf, Swedish author, first woman to win the Nobel Prize for Literature

1953 First Universal Children's Day, designated by the United Nations

25
1914 Birth date: Joseph Paul ("Joe") Di Maggio, baseball player

26
1922 Birth date: Charles Monroe Schulz, creator of *Peanuts*

27
1942 Birth date: Jimi Hendrix, rock guitarist

28
1757 Birth date: William Blake, English poet

Louisa May Alcott said:

"'Stay' is a charming word in a friend's vocabulary."

From the Latin word *novum, meaning "nine," November was the 9th month of the Roman calendar.*

FLOWER: CHRYSANTHEMUM
BIRTHSTONE: TOPAZ
ZODIAC SIGN: SAGITTARIUS, THE CENTAUR (NOVEMBER 22–DECEMBER 21)
SAGITTARIANS ARE GOOD-HUMORED AND FRIENDLY, AND THEY LOVE MEETING NEW PEOPLE. THEY ARE INTERESTED IN EVERYTHING AND EVERYBODY.

5
1968 Shirley Anita St. Hill Chisholm becomes the first African-American woman elected to the U.S. House of Representatives

6
1854 Birth date: John Philip Sousa, composer

7
1867 Birth date: Marie Sklodowska Curie, Polish-born French physicist, first person to win two Nobel prizes, 1903 and 1911

1967 Carl B. Stokes in Cleveland, Ohio, and Richard G. Hatcher in Gary, Indiana, become first two African-American mayors elected in major U.S. cities

1989 L. Douglas Wilder elected governor of Virginia, first African-American U.S. governor

8
1656 Birth date: Edmund Halley, English astronomer

1889 Montana: 41st state to enter the Union

13
1850 Birth date: Robert Louis Balfour Stevenson, Scottish author, poet

14
1765 Birth date: Robert Fulton, inventor

1840 Birth date: Claude Oscar Monet, French artist

1948 Birth date: Charles Philip Arthur George (Prince Charles), prince of Wales

15
1887 Birth date: Georgia O'Keeffe, artist

1897 Birth date: David McCord, poet

16
1907 Oklahoma: 46th state to enter the Union

21
1789 North Carolina: 12th state to enter the Union

22
1942 Birth date: Guion (Guy) Stewart Bluford, Jr., first African-American astronaut

23
1804 Birth date: Franklin Pierce, 14th U.S. president

1897 Pencil sharpener patented by John Lee Love

24
1784 Birth date: Zachary Taylor, 12th U.S. president

1826 Birth date: Carlo Lorenzini ("Carlo Collodi"), Italian author of *Pinocchio*

1864 Birth date: Henri de Toulouse-Lautrec, French artist

29
1832 Birth date: Louisa May Alcott, author of *Little Women*

1898 Birth date: Clives Staples ("C. S.") Lewis, British author of *Chronicles of Narnia* series

30
1835 Birth date: Samuel Langhorne Clemens, ("Mark Twain"), author of *The Adventures of Tom Sawyer*

1924 Birth date: Shirley Anita St. Hill Chisholm, first African-American congresswoman, candidate for U.S. presidency

WEATHER REPORT
On November 20, 1979, a blizzard struck Cheyenne, Wyoming, producing 19.8 inches of snow in 24 hours and a total of 25.6 inches in 40 hours.

If it is raining today, drivers and riders will thank Mary Anderson for this invention, registered as patent no. 743,801.

Windshield Wipers
Rebecca Kai Dotlich

Squishy, squish,
squeegy-squish,
tossing rain
side   to   side;
squish, squish,
squeegy-squish,
   flap
   flap,
puddle glide.
Slosh, slosh,
sloshing wash,
plish, plish,
tidal toss.
Squeegy-squish,
squish-squish, sway . . .

a perfect windshield
wiper day.

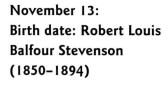

November 13:
Birth date: Robert Louis
Balfour Stevenson
(1850–1894)

Born in Edinburgh, Scotland,
Stevenson wrote classic novels,
including *Treasure Island* and
*The Strange Case of Dr. Jekyll
and Mr. Hyde*. His book of poetry
A Child's Garden of Verses is as
popular today as it was when it first
appeared in 1885, more than 115
years ago.

Windy Nights

Robert Louis Stevenson

Whenever the moon and stars are set,
    Whenever the wind is high,
All night long in the dark and wet,
    A man goes riding by.
Late in the night when the fires are out,
Why does he gallop and gallop about?

Whenever the trees are crying aloud,
    And ships are tossed at sea,
By, on the highway, low and loud,
    By at the gallop goes he.
By at the gallop he goes, and then
By he comes back at the gallop again.

National Children's Book Week

An event celebrated since 1919 heralds the wonders of books and reading. It is held each year the week before Thanksgiving. In 1973, Richard Armour wrote this Book Week Poem:

Two Lives Are Yours

Richard Armour

Books I think
Are extra nice.
Through books you live
Not once but twice.

You are yourself
And you are things
With fur or fins
Or shells or wings,

As big as giants
Small as gnats
As far as stars
As close as cats.

You live today
And long ago
The future, too,
Is yours to know.

You're multiplied,
Expanded, freed.
You're you and also
What you read.

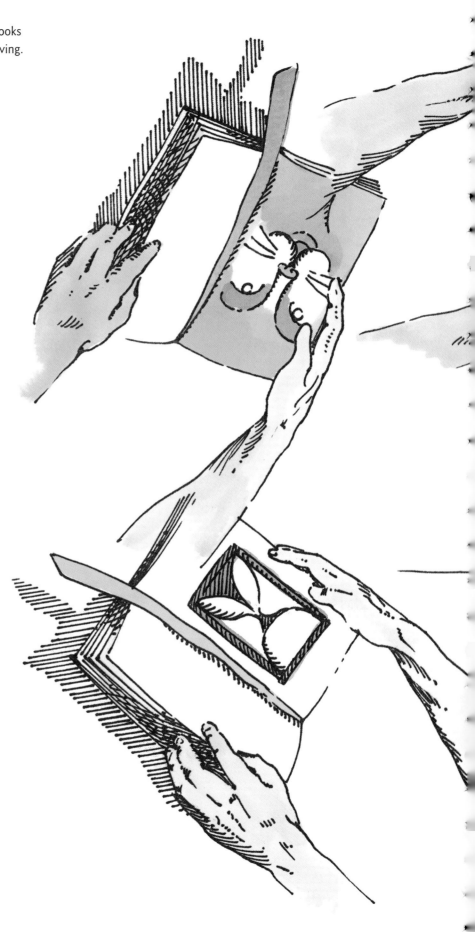

Thanksgiving Day

Because of the prodding of Sarah Josepha Buell Hale, author of "Mary Had a Little Lamb," President Abraham Lincoln issued a proclamation in 1864 to make the last Thursday in November Thanksgiving Day.

Thanksgiving *Anonymous*

The year has turned its circle,
The seasons come and go.
The harvest is all gathered in
And chilly north winds blow.

Orchards have shared their treasures,
The fields, their yellow grain,
So open wide the doorway—
Thanksgiving comes again!

Each year, by presidential proclamation, Native American Heritage Month is designated to honor the approximate 1.9 million Native Americans living in the United States today.

Iroquois Prayer *Anonymous*

We return thanks to our mother, the earth,
 which sustains us.
We return thanks to the rivers and streams,
 which supply us with water.
We return thanks to all herbs, which furnish
 medicines for the cure of our diseases.
We return thanks to the corn, and to her sisters,
 the beans and squashes, which give us life.
We return thanks to the bushes and trees,
 which provide us with fruit.
We return thanks to the wind, which,
 moving the air, has banished diseases.
We return thanks to the moon and stars,
 which have given to us their light
 when the sun was gone.
We return thanks to our grandfather Hé-no,
 that he has protected his grandchildren from
 witches and reptiles, and has given to us his rain.
We return thanks to the sun, that he has looked upon
 the earth with a beneficent eye.
Lastly, we return thanks to the Great Spirit,
 in whom is embodied all goodness, and who
 directs all things for the good of his children.

December

Kwanzaa: 7-day celebration, December 26–January 1, to honor the importance of African-American community and family

1 **1913** First drive-in gasoline station opened, Pittsburgh, PA	**2** **1859** Birth date: Georges Pierre Seurat, French artist	**3** **1818** Illinois: 21st state to enter the Union	**4** **1905** Birth date: Munro Leaf, author of *The Story of Ferdinand*
9 **1848** Birth date: Joel Chandler Harris, author of *Uncle Remus* series	**10** **1817** Mississippi: 20th state to enter the Union **1830** Birth date: Emily Elizabeth Dickinson, poet **1851** Birth date: Melvil Dewey, educator, inventor of Dewey decimal book system	**11** **1816** Indiana: 19th state to enter the Union	**12** **1787** Pennsylvania: 2nd state to enter the Union
17 **1843** *A Christmas Carol* by Charles Dickens published	**18** **1787** New Jersey: 3rd state to enter the Union	**19** **1732** *Poor Richard's Almanack* by Benjamin Franklin published	**20** **1985** U.S. poet laureate established by the Library of Congress
25 *Christmas Day* **1821** Birth date: Clarissa Harlowe ("Clara") Barton, humanitarian, founder of the American Red Cross	**26** **1898** Radium discovered by Pierre and Marie Curie, French scientists	**27** **1822** Birth date: Louis Pasteur, French chemist-bacteriologist, whose work led to the process of pasteurization	**28** **1846** Iowa: 29th state to enter the Union **1856** Birth date: Woodrow Wilson, 28th U.S. president

Emily Dickinson said:

"The Brain—is wider than the Sky—"

From the Latin word decem, *meaning "tenth," December was the 10th month in the Roman calendar.*

FLOWER: NARCISSUS
BIRTHSTONE: TURQUOISE
ZODIAC SIGN: CAPRICORN, THE GOAT (DECEMBER 22–JANUARY 19)
CAPRICORNS ARE HARDWORKING, AMBITIOUS, AND RELIABLE. THEY HAVE A WITTY SENSE OF HUMOR.

5
1782 Birth date: Martin Van Buren, 8th U.S. president

1830 Birth date: Christina Georgina Rossetti, English poet

1901 Birth date: Walter Elias ("Walt") Disney, filmmaker

6
1886 Birth date: (Alfred) Joyce Kilmer, poet

7
1787 Delaware: 1st state to enter the Union

8
1765 Birth date: Eli Whitney, inventor

13
1835 Birth date: Phillips Brooks, composer of "O Little Town of Bethlehem"

14
1819 Alabama: 22nd state to enter the Union

1897 Birth date: Margaret Chase Smith, first woman to serve in both the U.S. House of Representatives and Senate

15
1832 Birth date: (Alexandre) Gustave Eiffel, French engineer

1903 Ice-cream cone patented by Italo Marchiony

16
1770 Birth date: Ludwig van Beethoven, German composer

21
First day of winter

Chester Greenwood Day, celebrated in Maine in honor of the man who patented earmuffs

1620 The *Mayflower* anchored at Plymouth Rock in Plymouth, MA

22
1858 Birth date: Giacomo Puccini, Italian composer

1956 Birth date: Colo, the world's first gorilla born in captivity, Columbus Zoo, Columbus, OH

23
Night of the Radishes, La Noche de los Rabanos
Holiday celebrated in Oaxaca, Mexico

24
1871 Giuseppe Verdi's *Aida* premiered, Cairo, Egypt

29
1808 Birth date: Andrew Johnson, 17th U.S. president

1845 Texas: 28th state to enter the Union

1876 Birth date: Pablo Casals, Spanish cellist

30
1865 Birth date: Rudyard Kipling, English author of *The Jungle Book*

1975 Birth date: Eldrick ("Tiger") Woods, golfer

31
New Year's Eve
1869 Birth date: Henri Matisse, French artist

WEATHER REPORT
On December 8, 1938, the temperature at La Mesa, California, soared to 100 degrees, setting a United States record for the month of December.

December 21: First day of winter

I Heard a Bird Sing

Oliver Herford

I heard a bird sing

In the dark of December

A magical thing

And sweet to remember:

"We are nearer to Spring

Than we were in September,"

I heard a bird sing

In the dark of December.

December 21: Chester Greenwood Day

"My ears have always troubled me more or less, and I consequently had my mind fixed upon some invention with which I might protect them," said Chester Greenwood, born in Maine.

Greenwood did something about his freezing ears. At the age of 18, on March 13, 1877, he received patent no. 188,292 for his Greenwood Champion Ear Protectors, known as earmuffs. He set up a factory in Maine, and eventually sold more than 400,000 pairs, making Farmington, Maine, the earmuff capital of the world.

In 1997, 110 years after Greenwood received the patent, the Maine legislature declared December 21, the first day of winter, Chester Greenwood Day.

Muffs
Lee Bennett Hopkins

When

winter winds

begin to

howl

begin to

blast

begin to

growl—

when

winter winds

become

too gruff

it's time

to wear

a pair

of

muffs.

105

December 23: Night of the Radishes

In Oaxaca, Mexico, radishes grow larger than some yams. Since the 19th century Mexicans have carved sculptures out of the vegetable for an annual radish sculpture competition, La Noche de los Rabanos. Finished works are displayed in the zocalo, or town square. The best one wins a prize.

From
Near
the Window Tree

Karla Kuskin

Write about a radish.

Too many people write about the moon.

The night is black

The stars are small and high

The clock unwinds its ever-ticking tune

Hills gleam dimly

Distant nighthawks cry.

A radish rises in the waiting sky.

December 31: New Year's Eve

The Year

Felice Holman

goes
skidding
down
to
the
bottom
of the
cal-
en
dar
slip-
ping
out   **HAPPY NEW YEAR!**
the   top
end.   the
Then   to
ZOOM . . . . UP

109

Acknowledgments

Thanks are due to the following for permission to reprint selections:

Geoff Armour for "Two Lives Are Yours" by Richard Armour. Used by permission of Geoff Armour, who controls all rights.

Boyds Mills Press for "The River Is a Piece of Sky" from *The Reason for the Pelican* by John Ciardi. Copyright © 1994 by the family of John Ciardi; "Windshield Wipers" from *In the Spin of Things* by Rebecca Kai Dotlich. Text copyright © 2003 by Rebecca Kai Dotlich. Both reprinted by permission of Wordsong, Boyds Mills Press, Inc.

Joseph Bruchac for "In the Moon of Falling Leaves." Used by permission of the author, who controls all rights.

Children's Better Health Institute for "Earth, What Will You Give Me?" by Beverly McLoughland. From *Humpty Dumpty's Magazine,* copyright © 1977 by Parents' Magazines Enterprises. Used by permission of Children's Better Health Institute, Benjamin Franklin Literary & Medical Society, Inc., Indianapolis, Indiana.

Curtis Brown, Ltd., for "Fossil Finds." Copyright © 1995 by Rebecca Kai Dotlich. First appeared *Small Talk: A Book of Short Poems,* edited by Lee Bennett Hopkins, published by Harcourt, Inc.; "A Father's Hands" and "Treasure Words" copyright © 2005 by Rebecca Kai Dotlich; "A Question for Martin" copyright © 2005 by Nikki Grimes; "Subways Are People" copyright © 1971 by Lee Bennett Hopkins. First appeared in *Faces and Places: Poems for You,* published by Scholastic, Inc.; "The Ringmaster" copyright © 1982 by Lee Bennett Hopkins. First appeared in *Circus! Circus!,* published by Alfred A. Knopf, Inc.; "Soccer" copyright © 1996 by Lee Bennett Hopkins. First appeared in *Opening Days,* published by Harcourt, Inc.; "If You Believe Me" copyright © 1992 by Lee Bennett Hopkins. First appeared in *Ring Out, Wild Bells,* published by Harcourt, Inc.; "Muffs" copyright © 2005 by Lee Bennett Hopkins; "Wishing for Winter in Summer" copyright © 1991 by X. J. Kennedy. First appeared in *The Kite That Braved Old Orchard Beach,* published by Margaret K. McElderry Books; "Spring" copyright © 1983 by Prince Redcloud. All reprinted by permission of Curtis Brown, Ltd.

Faber and Faber Limited for "The Naming of Cats" from *Old Possum's Book of Practical Cats* by T. S. Eliot. Copyright © 1939 by T. S. Eliot and renewed 1967 by Esme Valerie Eliot. Canadian rights used by permission of Faber and Faber Limited.

Maria Fleming for "Groundhog." Used by permission of the author, who controls all rights.

Harcourt, Inc., for an excerpt from *More Opposites,* copyright © 1991 by Richard Wilbur; "The Naming of Cats" from *Old Possum's Book of Practical Cats,* copyright © 1939 by T. S. Eliot and renewed 1967 by Esme Valerie Eliot; "Arithmetic" from *The Complete Poems of Carl Sandburg,* copyright © 1970, 1969 by Lilian Steichen Sandburg, Trustee. All reprinted by permission of Harcourt, Inc.

HarperCollins Publishers for "Skipper" from *Bronzeville Boys and Girls* by Gwendolyn Brooks. Copyright © 1956 by Gwendolyn Brooks Blakely; "Freedom!" from *We the People* by Bobbi Katz. Copyright © 2000 by Bobbi Katz. Both used by permission of HarperCollins Publishers.

Felice Holman for "The Year" from *The Song in My Head* by Felice Holman. Charles Scribner's Sons, 1985. Used by permission of the author, who controls all rights.

Henry Holt and Company for "Blue-Butterfly Day" from *The Poetry of Robert Frost,* edited by Edward Connery Lathem. Copyright 1923, © 1969 by Henry Holt and Company, copyright 1951 Robert Frost. Reprinted by permission of Henry Holt and Company, LLC.

Constance Andrea Keremes for "Memorial Day." Used by permission of the author, who controls all rights.

Liveright for "hist whist" from *Complete Poems: 1904–1962* by E. E. Cummings, edited by George J. Firmage. Copyright 1923, 1951, © 1991 by the Trustees for the E. E. Cummings Trust. Copyright © 1976 by George James Firmage. Used by permission of Liveright Publishing Corporation.

Beverly McLoughland for "Pencils." Used by permission of the author, who controls all rights.

Jane Medina for "Me x 2/Yo x 2." Used by permission of the author, who controls all rights.

Penguin Group (USA), Inc., for "First Lady of Twentieth-Century Sports: Mildred 'Babe' Didrikson Zaharias" from *A Burst of Firsts: Doers, Shakers and Record Breakers* by J. Patrick Lewis, illustrated by Brian Ajhar, copyright © 2001 by J. Patrick Lewis. Used by permission of Dial Books for Young Readers, A Division of Penguin Young Readers Group, A Member of Penguin Group (USA), Inc., 345 Hudson Street, New York, New York 10014. All rights reserved.

Random House, Inc. for "Mother to Son" and "My People" from *The Collected Poems of Langston Hughes* by Langston Hughes, copyright © 1994 by The Estate of Langston Hughes. Used by permission of Alfred A. Knopf, a division of Random House, Inc.

Marci Ridlon for "Labor Day." Used by permission of the author, who controls all rights.

Joyce Carol Thomas for "Remembering Marian Anderson." Used by permission of the author, who controls all rights.

Scott Treimel NY for "Write About a Radish" from *Near the Window Tree* by Karla Kuskin. Copyright © 1975, 1980 by Karla Kuskin. Reprinted by permission of Scott Treimel NY.

The University of Arkansas Press for "Introduction to Poetry" from *The Apple that Astonished Paris* by Billy Collins. Copyright © 1988 by Billy Collins. Reprinted by permission of the University of Arkansas Press.

Janet S. Wong for "Prayer for the Lunar New Year." Used by permission of the author, who controls all rights.

Index of Titles

Index of First Lines

*I*ndex of Authors